FOOTBALL AND INTEGRATION IN PLANO, TEXAS

STAY IN THERE, WILDCATS!

The Plano Conservancy for Historic Preservation, Inc.

Foreword by Billy Ray Smith | Introduction by Robert Haynes

Charleston London

THE History PRESS

Published by The History Press
Charleston, SC 29403
www.historypress.net

First published 2014

Manufactured in the United States

ISBN 978.1.62619.501.1

Library of Congress CIP data applied for.

This book is dedicated to the many educators, coaches, community members and others who were instrumental in making integrated education a reality for Plano and beyond. Your vision, determination and passion are an inspiration to all of us.

Wildcat decal. *Courtesy of the Steve Christie Collection, Haggard Library, Plano, Texas.*

The Plano Wildcats state championship sign. *Courtesy of* The Planonian.

PLANO SENIOR HIGH SCHOOL FIGHT SONG

Stay in There, Wildcats

Stay in there, Wildcats
Do not let them pass
Stay in there, Wildcats
Show them you are fast
Show them who you are, boys
Fight them to the end
Stay in there, Wildcats
You're sure to win!

Stay in there, Wildcats
Do not let them pass
Stay in there, Wildcats
Show them you are fast
If they block your way, boys
Hit 'em hard and low
Stay in there, Wildcats
Fight for old Plano!

CONTENTS

FOREWORD

All of the young men with whom I played were exactly the same—we were all Plano Wildcats. No black, no white—just maroon.

The experience of growing up in Plano, Texas, was a dominant force in shaping the rest of my life.

In 1971, my Dad, Billy Ray Smith Sr., had just played his last game as a Baltimore Colt, and that game just happened to be Super Bowl V (Colts 16, Cowboys 13). Dad played in an era that didn't afford most players the luxury of training for six months before the NFL season kicked off. For the most part, the players had off-season jobs. Dad worked as a stockbroker for Alex Brown and Sons during the off-seasons in Baltimore. Upon his retirement from pro football, he accepted a similar position with White Weld & Company.

The White Weld office was in Dallas, Texas. So after beating the Cowboys in the Super Bowl, Dad did some homework and decided that Plano would be the perfect Dallas suburb in which to start his post-NFL life.

Not sure if he gave much thought of moving his family of six (I have a big brother and two sisters) to the city that he and his fellow Colts had pillaged for their only Super Bowl win, but I do know that he had nearby Plano High School on his mind when we moved into a two-story house on three acres in Ranch Estates. The Wildcats had two state titles (1965, 1967) and would tack on another the year we moved in (1971).

Billy Ray Smith Jr. *Courtesy of University of Arkansas.*

Plano was absolutely exploding as we were getting acclimated to our new home (and some pretty thick Texas accents). I finished the fourth grade in Miss Betty Hamby's classroom.

Barron Elementary opened the next year, and my fifth- and sixth-grade years went well, thanks to Miss Slama, Mrs. Dickey, Miss Ratcliffe and Miss Sandlin.

After a couple years playing PSA football, I thought I was ready to take the next step at Bowman Junior High.

The responsibility and privilege of playing in the Plano Wildcat system was understood by every player and coach. The legendary John Clark had put in place great coaches throughout the city. Every one of these coaches taught from the same playbook with the same focus. As the student-athletes would advance from level to level and school to school, they were all doing so with the same playbook, one that would get just a little thicker every year.

The training program was years ahead of any other in the state of Texas. Form running, quick drill exercises and even tumbling training were included in the program. We did not lift heavy; we lifted fast. We were operating with the belief that the work we were doing in the spring would pay off during the fall—and it did.

All of the young men with whom I played were exactly the same—we were all Plano Wildcats. No black, no white—just maroon.

After the '76 season, Coach Clark decided to hang up his whistle. We were incredibly lucky that Coach Kimbrough stepped in and took charge for the next two seasons (25-3-2). Playing for the state championship in '77 and '78 was possible because of the outstanding coaches and players who were willing to work and sacrifice to reach a goal. The fans who accompanied us for those two seasons were also a huge part of our success. Road trips to Waco or Odessa were easy because the ride back was as a winner. The last road trip we took was the one that hurt the most (losing to Houston Stratford in the Astrodome).

Ronny Hart, Roy "Bulldog" Stone, Robert Woods, Andy Coleman, Basil Clarke and Don Vardell—these men (and all the other coaches along the way) made it possible to achieve my goals on the football field, and I will be forever grateful for the experience of growing up a Plano Wildcat.

The guys who I lined up with every Friday night—Kevin Rush, C.M. Pier, Mike Pedigo, Steve Ulmer, Stevie Haynes, Kevin Jennings, Dave Chulick, Rick Stolle, Tim Lassiter, Hans Mansion, Kevin Jennings, Carl Smith and Ricky Gaddis, to name a few—will always be champions.

My apologies to the teammates I didn't list, as well as the cheerleaders, the drill team (Planoettes) and the marching band—I wasn't given nearly enough room to properly thank you for your contributions. Just know that I consider us all a part of one of the greatest teams that Texas high school football has ever seen.

—Billy Ray Smith

About Billy Ray Smith

Billy Ray Smith attended Plano Senior High School and in 1977 helped the Plano Wildcats claim the Texas state championship. While attending the University of Arkansas, Smith was a consensus All-American in 1981 and

1982. He is a member of the Arkansas Razorback All-Century Team, the Arkansas State Hall of Fame and the College Football Hall of Fame.

In 1983, the San Diego Chargers made Billy the fifth overall pick and the first defensive pick in the NFL draft. Smith would play his entire ten-year NFL career with the Chargers. He was the Chargers' defensive player of the year in 1985 and 1986 and San Diego's MVP in 1987. Smith was named Second-Team All-AFC in 1986 and 1987 and was voted Second-Team All-Pro in 1989. He was also voted one of the fifty greatest Chargers of all time.

Smith's father was also a football standout. Billy Ray Smith Sr. played for the Arkansas Razorbacks and spent thirteen years in the NFL playing for the Los Angeles Rams, Pittsburgh Steelers and Baltimore Colts.

ACKNOWLEDGEMENTS

We extend our gratitude to Maggie Sprague and Russell Kissick, the co-founders of the Plano Conservancy for Historic Preservation, Inc., for their dedication to preserving Plano's heritage for future generations and for their unending support of many outstanding historic preservation projects. We are inspired by your tireless dedication and firm commitment to telling the story of the history of Plano.

Thank you to the Plano Conservancy for Historic Preservation, Inc. Board of Directors—Russell Kissick, Jeff Campbell, Candace Fountoulakis, Harry Kepner, Duane Peter, Pete Schoemann, Sidney Wall, Amy Sandling Crawford, Clint Haggard, Lauren Partovi and Barbara Zepeda—for your support of this project.

We would also like to thank Plano Independent School District athletic director Gerald Brence as well as the current and past legends of Plano Independent School District athletics for taking the time to share their stories with us. Your legacies will not be forgotten.

We also pause to acknowledge the kindness of Cheryl Smith of the Plano Public Library System. Thank you for allowing us to use many images from the W.O. Haggard Jr. Library Genealogy, Local History, Texana and Archives collection.

Thanks as well to the Baylor University Institute for Oral History for its assistance with this project. The institute's "Getting Started with Oral History" workshop provided our team with valuable instruction and resources necessary for success in gathering information.

We also extend special thanks to the City of Plano for its generosity and support. Plano's rich history and bright future are part of an ongoing story that we will continually strive to relay to longtime residents and newcomers alike. In all things, Plano truly is a "City of Excellence."

INTRODUCTION

Back in 1960, when I was a young man of nineteen, I walked a picket line with my father, Sammie Haynes, a former baseball player for the Kansas City Monarchs. Having lost his sight to glaucoma, his career had been cut short midway, but not his enthusiasm and love for the game and his baseball buddies. He loved both baseball and football and kept up with all the scores and statistics nationwide.

As a former player for the Negro Leagues, he often shared with the family many stories of his days of triumph and excitement in baseball. He hated the discrimination and Jim Crow practices that he and his teammates faced as they toured the country playing ball. But he loved the game and the standing it brought him from African Americans everywhere the team went.

Dad asked me and other sportsmen and fans, including some former Negro League players, to join him in front of the Los Angeles Coliseum for an organized protest and picket line against the Washington Redskins football team, which was scheduled to play the annual charity game for Boys Clubs against the Los Angeles Rams that day. The Washington Redskins' owner, George P. Marshall, had refused to hire and put a black player on the team in spite of many 1950s and '60s social and political pressures.

As the winds of change blew harder throughout professional sports, the American Nazi Party had demonstrated its support of Marshall's Redskins with a picket line in front of the stadium in Washington, D.C., to "Keep the Redskins White."

Our picket group assembled at the appointed time in front of the main entrance to the coliseum that morning. I looked at my father, who was standing very tall with his chest out and having friendly conversation with other men as if they were in a locker room—just as they had done so many times in their careers. Dad needed me to hold a picket placard and walk in front of him on the line while he walked behind me with his left hand on my shoulder to guide himself as he held the placard stick with his right hand.

I stood with Dad in a friendly and athletic group watching as he greeted and talked with other men he knew, men who knew and understood the real meaning of our being there. While not being included in their conversations, I noticed how my father was holding his picket sign. I don't remember what the signs said, but I held my picket sign in a clenched fist. My father also held his with a clenched fist, but he used his thumb to brace the stick from behind. The straightness of his thumb was the same as the straightness of his back, with both the thumb and his back being slightly arched. It seemed that his thumb rising from his clenched fist and his standing so tall were delivering a message of pride and defiance rather than what was printed on the picket sign itself.

The demonstration went well, and one more gust was added to the winds of change that were continuing to blow through America. The assault on the citadel of discrimination, racism and Jim Crow in sports begun by Jackie Robinson and Branch Rickey in 1947 continued apace into the 1950s and '60s. The signal event of the Birmingham Bus Boycott captured attention throughout the nation, especially the South, and must have presaged things to come for watchful eyes and listening ears in Texas.

Actually, in 1958, the Redskins had inadvertently drafted a black player when draftee Alphonso Thompson, from Lincoln University in St. Louis, signed a contract with the team that had been sent to him by mail (it was never clear how this occurred or who sent the offer). However, when Alphonso showed up for training camp at Occidental College in Southern California with contract in hand and ready to begin training, no one could explain what a black player was doing there. News reporters on the scene sought out southern-born George Preston Marshall, who came down to the field dressed in a white suit and wearing a wide-brim white straw hat and said to Alphonso: "Son, I don't have anything against you, but you are a nigger, and I will never have a nigger on my team as long as I am the owner!"

George Preston Marshall's team was the last NFL team to remain segregated up and into the 1960s.

But the tides of change in major-league sports could no longer be ignored when newly elected President John F. Kennedy, through his secretary of the

Newly elected President John F. Kennedy discussing the integration of the Washington Redskins with Morris Udall. *Library of Congress.*

interior, Morris Udall, advised Marshall that the segregated Washington Redskins team would not be allowed to play in the new Department of the Interior–owned stadium in Washington, D.C., (the capital of the free world) unless he hired a Negro ballplayer. Marshall, having resisted all pressures to integrate his team, responded that he would hire a Negro player when the Department of the Interior hired more than its one Negro park ranger. Udall then immediately directed that several Negro national park rangers be hired.

George Preston Marshall understood clearly that, without a stadium in which to play, his Redskins would start to lose money, and as Robert Frost so aptly and clearly stated in his poem "Money," "when money speaks, all the world is silent." In 1962, Marshall brought two Negro players onto the team and had one of his best seasons. However, attempting to reach out from the grave, in his will he left a large sum of money to orphans in Washington, D.C., with instructions that none of it was to go to any minority children. This directive was overturned by court order, and the money was shared by all orphans in the city.

Tragic events in Alabama and Mississippi in 1963, the major urban riots in Brooklyn in 1964 and Los Angeles in 1965 and unrest throughout the South that had begun in the 1960s finally aroused a nation to seek change and live up to its creed. In Texas, faced with the momentum of changing events, especially those arising from the 1954 school desegregation decision, Plano high school coaches began to examine their options to deal with the inevitable.

In June 1898, "whitecaps" attempted to turn Plano into a "sundown town" by forcing out all the "colored" citizens. A mysterious series of postings written in pencil on cardboard and posted throughout the small town warned all "coloreds" to leave "or else." Some families did leave, but Mayor Farlin called a meeting with the town council and decided that such lawlessness would not be allowed to prevail in the small community and that all citizens must be protected. A group of men was deputized to patrol the city at night and to be on the lookout for any threats to these "colored" citizens.

From the 1898 series of whitecap incidents, Plano evolved an attitude of acceptance of its Negro residents and began to treat them with a margin of respect that was not common in Texas and certainly not in other parts of the South. Plano's "coloreds" likewise prospered along with the rest of the city's residents in an atmosphere of mutual respect and acceptance. And although Plano's residential segregation grew as the small frontier town grew into an important suburb of Dallas, and the Douglass community within it emerged as Plano's "colored district," acceptance and mutual respect between blacks and whites remained undiminished as the twentieth century unfolded.

Plano's high school athletic coaches always knew that athletic ability is no respecter of groups or individuals. It visits and comes to stay with those who have a vision and are willing to work hard. Thus, coaches who wanted to win looked for and recognized ability and strove to create a climate where it could develop freely by fostering respect for the individual and hard work to achieve excellence.

In looking back, the secret to Plano's success in peacefully integrating its high school athletic programs was no secret at all. It was common sense.

—Robert Haynes

About Robert Haynes

Robert Haynes is curator at the Plano Interurban Railway Museum and director of the Johnny J. Myers Archives and Research Center in Plano. Trained as an anthropologist at the University of California–Berkeley and in museum studies at San Francisco State University, he recently co-authored the book *Plano and the Interurban Railway*.

Robert Haynes, author and curator. *Courtesy of Robert Haynes.*

He has also studied and done research at the Université de Bordeaux in Talence, France, as well as the Université du Benin in Togo and the University of Ghana–Legon. He has studied at the Smithsonian's National Museum of American History and received an appointment to study at the Getty Museum Management Institute.

As founding director of the African American Museum and Library at Oakland, California, he was managing editor of the publication *From the Archives* and created the groundbreaking exhibit "Bittersweet Triumph: African Americans in World War II," which was recognized by the Associated Press.

Recruited to come to Dallas as deputy director of the Dallas African American Museum, he later chose to explore his interest in trains and rail technology by accepting the position as curator of the Interurban Railway Museum.

Mr. Haynes is also chief curator and director of Texas Curatorial Services in Dallas, having served clients such as the Old Red Courthouse Museum, the Irving History Center, the Mayme Clayton Museum of California and the Dallas African American Museum, and personally specializes in voice-overs for museums.

In addition to his expertise in museum management, Mr. Haynes brings to the history of electric rail in North Texas a humanistic perspective that takes on social change and process. He is dedicated to preserving the memory and knowledge of the electric interurban system in North Texas.

Chapter 1
IN THE BEGINNING

This is much more than a story about the integration of a football team. This is the story of the community members, the business owners, the civic leaders, the football players, the cheerleaders, the students, the educators and the many others who were affected in many and various ways by a turbulent and memorable time in our country's history.

Class of 1922 football lettermen for Plano High School. *Courtesy of the Interurban Railway Museum Collection.*

Integration in Plano meant that black and white students were coming together not only in the classroom but also on the football field. Although school integration in Plano was a much smoother experience than integration in some other cities, the process was not without challenges and hiccups. High school integration came to Plano in 1964. And to the city's surprise and delight, the newly integrated football team won the first of the school's seven state championships the very next year in 1965.

This is a story that features many heroes and legends whose names will forever be remembered. It is a story of many emotions—crushing heartbreak, sheer happiness, guarded fear, terrible agony and overwhelming delight. This is a story of an amazing time in history, both for the city of Plano and for this country. This is a story about a time in Plano's history that should never be forgotten.

The Past

Today, the bustling metropolitan city of Plano, Texas, features a wealth of schools, a myriad of single-family homes and multifamily developments, the headquarters of many corporations, a wide variety of high-end shopping destinations, an array of lush parks and green spaces and much more.

And those green spaces and the occasional small farm or intermittent field of livestock around town give hints to the city's agricultural roots. Plano, Texas, was once a small farming community.

Initial efforts to settle the Collin County's blackland prairie began in 1841, but progress was stalled by confrontations with Native Americans until 1844. Settlements were widely scattered at that time, and only a few were made in 1845.[1]

In 1846, William Foreman bought Peter's Colony land from a gentleman named Sanford Beck and settled northeast of Plano. Plano's birth was due, in part, to the Foreman family. Foreman erected a sawmill and gristmill that were in high demand by his neighbors and many others in the area. A general store and cotton gin were soon added, and these popular facilities attracted many others to the area.[2]

In 1847, Joseph, Daniel and Samuel Klepper continued to expand the community. Silas Harrington, his brother Alfred and Dr. Henry Dye settled in the area in 1848. Dye was the first medical doctor in the settlement.

Mail service was established around 1850, and Foreman's home became the unofficial post office. As the area continued to grow, expand and mature, Dye felt the city needed a proper name. He sent an application to Washington, D.C., requesting that the city be named Fillmore in honor of the president of the United States.

The name Fillmore was rejected, and the name Foreman was suggested but declined by William Foreman. Dye was determined to have a community with a recognized name, so he suggested "Plano." He thought the word *plano* meant "plain" in Spanish, but it actually means "flat." Regardless of Plano's meaning, postal authorities approved the name, and Plano became the official name of the community. Not surprisingly, William Foreman served as the first postmaster.[3]

Plano was platted and incorporated in 1873 and elected a mayor and board of aldermen that same year. At first, Plano seemed to grow slowly, but the city experienced a population boom after World War II, eventually growing into the thriving suburb of today.

The city was affected by major fires in 1881 and 1895 that destroyed many of its buildings. Even though these violent fires repeatedly destroyed Plano's business district, the city's determined businessmen replaced older city structures and those damaged by fire with modern brick buildings.[4]

In 1881, the city assumed responsibility for what would eventually become Plano Independent School District (PISD), ending the days of Plano being served only by private schools.[5] The private Plano Institute opened in 1882 under the direction of W.F. Mister, and the private Plano Academy was developed under Matthew C. Portman. These private schools were later taken over by the public school system.

The education system in Plano enjoyed growth and expansion following the formation of the Plano public school system in 1891. Plano High School was created in 1952 to separate primary students from those in the higher grades. High school students from Plano at this time enjoyed a great degree of academic success, with a majority of graduating seniors going on to study in college.[6]

Population growth and the passage of time brought many changes to the area. Over time, Plano slowly shifted away from its agricultural heritage. Improvements in public works and residential and business development began to change the landscape of the city.

Expansion and development continued beyond the city's educational system. J. Crittenden and E.K. Rudolph began publishing Plano's first newspaper, the *Plano News*, in 1874. Early Plano industries included plumbing and stove plants, a garment factory and an electric-wire factory.[7]

Residents living in Plano between 1908 and 1948 had an opportunity to experience the rollicking, clickity-clack sway of riding on an Interurban Texas Electric Railway car. This second generation of rail transportation extended from Denison to Waco, with connections to Fort Worth, Cleburne and Denton possible through the hub station in Dallas.[8]

Rail transportation powered by steam first arrived in Plano in 1872 and forever changed the agrarian lifestyle of early settlers who had traveled to this area by covered wagon. While steam engines guaranteed the survival and likelihood of growth to a community and transported farm crops to distant locations, the laborious process of producing enough steam to drive the train forward limited the frequency of stops along a line. In the late 1880s, ingenious inventors discovered the wonder of electricity and devised ways to harness this marvel into driving trolley cars previously drawn by mules or horses.[9]

Entrepreneurs, capitalizing on ways to market this new transportation, developed systems throughout the United States that connected small towns and outlying farms to a large, regional city. Overnight, farming families isolated from society by distance had easy and affordable access to opportunities and amenities available to urban populations.[10]

Located in downtown Plano, the Texas Electric Railway Station served to bring people, goods, newspapers with worldwide coverage and traveling salesmen together in a timely fashion.[11] A contract signed with the U.S. Post Office in 1914 permitted mail to be carried and delivered to the many towns along the line via the Texas Electric Railway System. Three interurban cars were refitted with bins, sorting tables, mail slots and cancellation stamps enabling two postal employees, in a secured rear compartment, to process mail as the car traveled north and south on its daily schedule.[12]

Throughout much of the twentieth century, Plano continued to rely on the city's surrounding farms and ranches for its livelihood. When the U.S. population began to shift in the 1970s, Plano welcomed many newcomers to the area. Many were job transplants, bringing their families and their businesses from across the country and the globe. Plano became one of the fastest-growing cities in the United States.[13]

By the mid-1980s, Plano overtook McKinney as the commercial, financial and educational center of Collin County with an estimated one thousand businesses. At the time, Plano was the corporate home of the Frito-Lay Corporation, a satellite communication system and several computer manufacturers. By 1990, it was a city of seventy-two square miles with a population of 128,713.[14]

Today's historic downtown Plano gives residents and visitors a glimpse of days gone by. It features a quaint atmosphere, including brick streets and sidewalks and turn-of-the-century lampposts. The area has experienced several revitalization projects and features many residential housing options, specialty shops, boutiques, galleries and restaurants; a regional history museum; a scenic park with a pond, playground and gazebo; and close access to light-rail transportation.

Today's Plano is much changed from the city of just a generation ago, but the growth of the city and the nature of its spirit can be traced back to those first settlers who came to the area many years ago.[15]

The Place

Many African Americans settled in the Plano area following the Civil War.[16] Over time, African American men and women became successful in farming the land of the blackland prairie. Many African Americans in the area started businesses, owned automobiles and, over time, began to develop a sense of place and community. Business life, social life and education for children were somewhat segregated from white neighbors, but for the most part, the two groups seemed to co-exist peacefully. There were times when the lives and experiences of African Americans in the Plano area would overlap with those of their white neighbors, but when asked about that point in time in the community, most remember a generally harmonious atmosphere.

"The statutes of the state and mores of the country were that you didn't integrate, but we were already integrated personally and emotionally before Rosa Parks," said John Lewis, who played football in Plano prior to the city's school integration. "We were already an integrated community—how would we live separately? The black community was not a stranger to the white community, and the white community was not a stranger to the black community. I have often wondered why we didn't make an earlier attempt because it was there as long as I can remember in Plano, Texas. There was a bond and a relationship and a trust that always existed. Finally, someone opened the red sea for us. The idea that it could have happened in Plano long before it happened on the national scene."[17]

Alton Allman was raised in Plano and served as the city's mayor from 1962 to 1964, just prior to the high school's integration. "We used to go across the railroad tracks and back up to the Douglass community to play kickball with the black kids," he recalled. "Being around black people was never a problem. My mother and dad were very open-minded and never prejudiced, and I never heard them say a derogatory word toward the black people. It was just sort of a natural thing."[18]

Lewis recalled a few periods of discomfort during Plano's integration process. "We had [a little] friction in integration. But there are only two times I knew of. And I wasn't very smart, but I kept my head on a swivel. I knew my surroundings."[19] He remembered that at one point, some of Jim Thomas's (a patriarch of Plano's Douglass community) children had moved away from the Plano area, but several had stayed in town. "One of the Thomas boys came back in town. He had been living in California or somewhere else on the West Coast, and he came to the front door of the Dairy Queen and wanted service." The owner of the Dairy Queen at that time was a former Department of Public Safety trooper and still carried a firearm. "The Thomas boy came in and demanded service. In a threatening manner, he demanded service," recalled Lewis. The Dairy Queen owner retrieved his weapon and told the young man to get out. The young man left in such haste that he broke the glass in the door or the window.[20] "His father, Jim Thomas, found out and told him, 'Look, this is our home, this is our community. These people have helped you boys out—they are my family, they are my friends. If you are going to act like that, you are not welcome in my home.' As far as I know, nothing ever came of that," added Lewis.[21]

He recalled another incident in 1968, after he had graduated from high school. "When I was out of school, I heard there was going to be a rumble one night between the blacks and the whites. [But] someone interceded or calmer heads prevailed—I don't know what it was." And that was the end of the problem, he said.[22]

Alton Allman recalled an incident involving African American visitors coming to Plano from Dallas. "Prior to integration, there was a group of black guys that came into town from Dallas. They went to the Harrington Pharmacy and went in and demanded service. They were real arrogant and causing trouble. Art [the pharmacy owner] told his person working to serve them and then went and called Jim Thomas." Shortly thereafter, Jim Thomas and six or seven members of Plano's African American community came to the pharmacy and told the arrogant visitors to "get the hell out of town and never come back. [Jim] was really well respected on both sides. He came over and ran them out of town," said Allman.[23]

James Thomas recalls learning much about responsibility and human interactions from his grandfather, the revered Jim Thomas, who had many,

many friends in both the African American and white communities. "My grandfather was the custodian of all of downtown Plano," recalled James. "I cleaned banks and spittoons. I remember being eight years old doing that. My grandfather's expectation was that you will be respected if you respect others."[24]

Thomas said that the atmosphere in Plano and beyond in the 1960s surely must have had times of tension and strife but that he really doesn't remember much of that. "We had expectations. Our teachers were fabulous, and the coaches were fabulous," he said. "When we transferred to the white school, we had [wonderful teachers]. When we had an opportunity to play [football] because we were black—they had seen the white kids play—I was thinking that this couldn't happen. When we got our suits on and showed who we were and what we could do, we got that opportunity. The best players were on the field all the time."[25]

Even though there were slight rumblings of discontent and some minor race-related issues, big problems never really materialized, Lewis added. He said that for generations in Plano, residents of every color all seemed to work together to get along. "We were all poor. We were just common. I think Plano had been conditioned for that. There was no friction, no hostility, no violence. But that's the story. It had to be one of the most seamless integrations on record."[26]

Jack Williams lived in the Douglass community and admitted that although integration went well in Plano, it was not always smooth sailing. "We didn't have any problems when [the civil rights movement] was going on," he said. "After integration, we had several isolated incidents."[27] Williams admitted that the isolated incidents were a small price to pay for the overall progress that was enjoyed by everyone in the city. "Integration was great for our kids."[28] Jack's wife, Norma, recalled that not everyone in Plano embraced integration easily. "They were hanging scarecrows and burning crosses in yards here, too," she added.[29]

Ken Bangs was an influential player on the Plano football team from 1964 to 1966. When asked now about the time of integration in the mid-1960s, both in Plano and across the country, he remembers being proud of the way Plano handled integration when compared to other parts of the county. "My mother worked at the Duchess Café," he said. "When black people would come in, they would go to the kitchen and eat or pick up [food]. We were a small southern town. There was a separation. It would be a lie to say there was not. But there was not a living animosity. If you look back over the years, why are you surprised? Because that's the way it was. It seemed natural."[30]

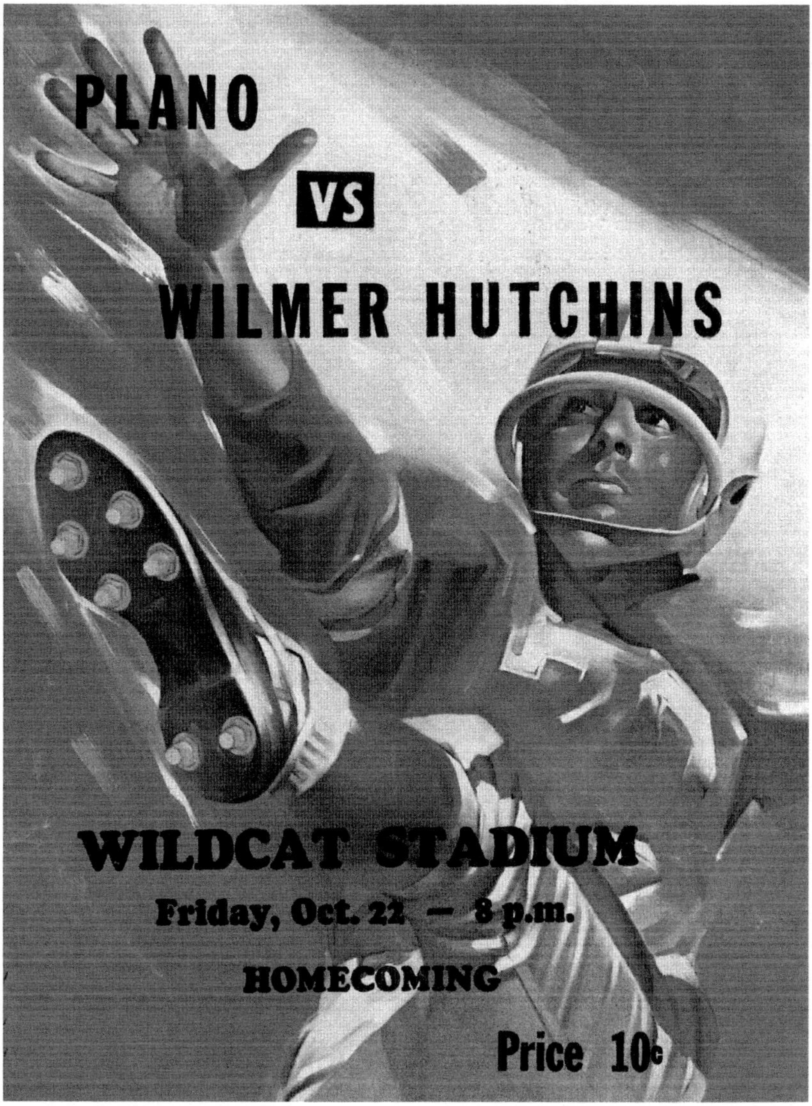

Game program for Plano vs. Wilmer Hutchins. *Courtesy of the Steve Christie Collection, Haggard Library, Plano, Texas.*

When Bangs attended college at the University of Texas–El Paso, which was then called Texas Western College, he recalled sitting in the living center of his dorm watching race-related riots on television. "It was a shock to me. We didn't have that kind of thing [here in Plano]. [But there] we were divided, and things were said…it was white against black."[31]

WILDCAT JOHN ROBINSON (30) fled down the field as Richardson's Craig Evans (21) and Eddie Matthews (53) darted to stop the ball carrier. Johnny Poole (right) scurried to assist in the play during the Wildcat-Lake Highland game last Friday night. (PHS Staff Photo by Norman Tietz)

Johnny Robinson during a game against Richardson. *Courtesy of the* Plano Star Courier.

"When I went to college…the year before, they had won the national championship with an all-black basketball team," he added. "And the racial tension! Football players lived in their own dorm. Basketball players lived in their own dorm. But the racial tension was so…even with the team it was so pronounced. When we traveled, there was a lot of racial tension with us taking lots of black players into the restaurants and hotels. Separation there was very strong. On the field, we performed together, but we weren't together. There was still a lot of resentment about the way the national championship was won. The coach purposely started five [African American] players and told the white players they were not going to play. That's not team."[32]

He recalled that when playing football in Plano, he and his teammates were always taught to be a cohesive unit and not to focus on one's self. "The guy next to you did his job or he didn't play," said Bangs. "It didn't matter who your daddy was. There were some moneyed people in town. They were on the team, and they were treated right. But they didn't star."[33]

But in college, things were different. "We had five number-one draft choices when I was a freshman," said Bangs. "All of them but one were black. George Daney played for Kansas City for about fifteen years. He was an offensive guard, and if you weren't careful, he would beat you on sprints."[34]

John Lewis recalled when he realized Plano was handling integration better than other parts of the country:

> *This was about 1965. I didn't play sports. I was working at TI* [Texas Instruments] *and went to school during the daytime. Montgomery* [Alabama] *and all of that was going on, and I just couldn't get my head wrapped around that. I just couldn't understand why that was going. You would see the national media—I just couldn't understand. A group of us T.I. white guys were going to the march. But I knew I'd lose my job if we went. But we were going down there because I knew it wasn't right. My sons—I have three sons—at home have never heard anything, any talk in a prejudiced manner because it's wrong. God made us all the same; he just made us all different colors. That's when I realized that we were living in a world different than everybody else.*[35]

"When I went into the army, I saw the difference there, too," added Lewis. "Talk about racial tensions! Plano was so unique. I think Plano is still unique. It's not...listen, this was the best place in the world to grow up. We were in a protected environment. It was not a real world."[36]

Chapter 2
THE STATE OF THINGS

Integration of school classrooms, football fields, locker rooms and communities was met with a wide variety of responses, and results ranged from cool acceptance to violent opposition all across the state of Texas and beyond. While one city seemed to integrate rather smoothly, its nearby neighbors might have been plagued with riots, protests or much worse. The emotional atmosphere during this time was super-charged, and integration experiences across the state of Texas were extremely varied.

Surrounding Cities

Frisco, Texas

Charlie Pearson was the president of the school board in Frisco, Texas, in 1965, when Plano High School integrated. At the time, Frisco had an elementary school in operation for children of color, but the city did not have any further education available for them. Frisco's African American students who wished to continue with their education were bussed to the Fredrick Douglass School in Plano, Texas.

When Plano voted to integrate students into one central high school, Frisco city officials had some major decisions to make. Pearson recalled the emotions and attitudes of the city and its people when it was discovered they would have to face the question of integration: "We had to do something with the kids—they all deserved an education."[37] Pearson said the decision to integrate the students inside of Frisco's district was an obvious solution that caused very few waves in the city and community.

Pearson grew up in Plano. As a young boy, he had a black friend. He recalled that every morning, the city's "white-only" school bus would drive by, and all of the children waved to one another. Pearson recalled that it seemed strange to him even then that the black and white students in the area didn't all go to the same school simply because both students being in the same schools would have been more efficient. His childhood experiences carried into his adult administrative career, as he eventually directed the Frisco School Board to integrate schools without incident.

Carrollton, Texas

Carrollton, Texas, which is located ten minutes west of Plano, integrated in 1963 due in large part to the efforts of Annie Heads Rainwater. Rainwater was born in 1912, and she loved to sew. She had multiple siblings and eventually multiple children who would be blocked from the public schools in the area because of the color of their skin. She was a civil rights activist and a proponent of integration.[38] She and her family received death threats and threats that their home would be burned down.[39]

One of Rainwater's sons said that his mother also lost friends because of her devotion to desegregation. She taught her children to "keep loving people despite what they do, and that makes you win." She also taught her children to be leaders and to lead people in the right direction.[40] In 1994, a Carrollton elementary school was opened and named in her honor.

A senior when R.L. Turner in Carrollton Texas integrated, Annie Spears Edwards remembers being "terrified."[41] In an interview, Edwards stated, "During my childhood, I have seen the Ku Klux Klan. And I was really frightened because I knew what was happening in Mississippi and Alabama, and I just knew we were going to get bombed."[42] Edwards, like other students of the era, had attended multiple schools before settling into R.L. Turner for her senior year. She was bussed to Booker T. Washington in downtown Dallas and then Fred Moore High School in Denton.

Dorothy Graves echoed Edward's sentiments. "It was something very new," she said, "it was very scary. I had never been around that many white people in my life because the only times that I would be around white people is when we went to school and that was it."[43]

Both Graves and Edwards said that despite their fears and the seeming chaos happening around the country, they never experienced it firsthand themselves at R.L. Turner High School.

Nancy Williams, daughter of Annie Heads Rainwater, said that at first "the students were overly helpful and friendly" but that by the second semester, everyone began to relax and settle in. The rest of the city followed in the school's footsteps. "Actually, if you stopped to think about it, once the school was integrated, the town just automatically integrated. All of a sudden, you could go in places you couldn't have before. It was just once it was done, it was done, for the most part."[44] The Carrollton-Farmers Branch Independent School District now has more than thirty-nine schools and more than twenty-six thousand students, all proudly and successfully diverse.

Garland, Texas

Garland, Texas, integrated in the 1960s in a relatively quiet manner due to a federal court order that remains in effect in 2014. The court order was modified in 1987 by the local NAACP chapter. In 2014, Garland Independent School District had fifty-eight students still under federal mandate for busing. Garland ISD utilizes a "pick your school" program. Town officials theorized that building quality institutions in older, core parts of the town would bring life back to these areas through the investments of parents and students. While this is a positive idea in theory, in practice, many students do not receive their first choice of schools and end up on bus rides that take more than forty minutes.

In 1967, John Washington was among the 689 black students integrated into the system when Garland ISD revealed its school choice program.[45] Washington experienced something the students in 2014 are still experiencing—the promise that a newer building equals a better education. Unfortunately, however, that is not always true. While there were not riots or even much press regarding the 1960s integration of Garland ISD, Washington remembers his "new" school having "Dixie" as its fight song, a colonel mascot and a plantation mural on the cafeteria wall.[46]

The NCAAP is still an integral force in guiding Garland ISD's integration efforts. Garland branch president Ricky McNeal submitted a written

McKinney High School football team, 1924. *Courtesy of North Texas History Center, Denton, Texas.*

statement on the issue in which he said, "Performance is the primary indicator of the overall success. Some of the data is good...we are on the correct course. However, there is still work to do."[47]

In 2014, a multi-ethnic committee acted to monitor community integration activity. The group sought to recruit minority teachers to boost interest in the magnet schools' offerings. As was true in the 1960s, the hope in 2014 was that the growth of magnet schools would match the growth of the population. Although it might be hard to believe, in 2014, Garland, Texas, was still under federal mandates regarding integration. This fact demonstrates that true integration is still not being fully achieved, even though efforts to integrate began more than forty years ago. However, it seems that the residents of Garland are not willing to give up on the subject and are working diligently to provide access to quality education for all students.

McKinney, Texas

Integration in McKinney was without major incident, but it did not mirror the mostly happy coming together of its neighbor to the south, Plano.

Leonard Evans, Iola Malvern and Jesse McGowen all have McKinney Independent School District schools named after them due to their tireless efforts not only toward integration but also the successful progression of their communities.[48] All three of these individuals were longtime residents of the city and witnessed the changes in the McKinney community firsthand.

In an interview, Leonard Evans stated he remembered being young and not being able to eat in the cafés.[49] He recalled that African Americans received the same quality of food as white guests and that business owners were polite and regarded African Americans as valued customers as long they did not break the race rules regarding where to sit and where to eat. "We were trained by our parents as to what we could do and what we couldn't," recalled Evans.[50] "Most blacks knew how far they could go." He recalled McKinney as being 100 percent segregated but said that people were used to it. "When you get in the habit of doing things, you don't consider it bad because it's something you do every day," he said.

Iola Malvern echoed Evans's sentiments regarding the Ritz Theatre in town. "You could go there any day you wanted, and they didn't bother you. But you had to go up to the balcony, and you could only sit on one side," she said.[51] She recalled that sometimes the section would get full, and people would have to stand even though there were open seats in different sections of the theater. Malvern drew the line at that point, stating that "I wasn't going to be standing on no wall just to see a picture."[52]

Leonard Evans was the principal and football coach at the E.S. Doty School in the 1960s. When the McKinney Independent School District integrated in 1966, he became the first black man to teach at a traditionally all-white school in the district. He also became the first black man on the McKinney Independent School District school board, a post he would hold until 2005.[53]

Iola Malvern was a McKinney Independent School District schoolteacher for thirty years. She said that throughout her years as a teacher, the classroom seemed a little bit harder on black men than it was on black women. "I never had that much of a problem. It seemed that a lot of people were kind of reluctant about having a black man teaching their girls."[54]

Jesse McGowan agreed. During an interview, he recalled being out in the community one time and having a group of fathers loudly inform one another that they did not want a black man teaching their daughters. McGowan understood them to be talking specifically so that he could hear them. Over the next few years, some of those same parents ended up requesting that their children be transferred into McGowan's class. "I guess we had to prove ourselves," he said.[55]

Major Cities

Fort Worth, Texas

An hour west of Plano and thirty-two miles west of Dallas is the major city of Fort Worth, Texas. Integration did not occur without incident in Fort Worth. One of the major differences between Fort Worth and Dallas was that Fort Worth did not have residential segregation in the same way that Dallas did. While most of the white population in Dallas lived north of Interstate 30. In Fort Worth, however, the black streets were next to the white streets, and the black neighborhoods were next to the white neighborhoods. This proximity required that any questions regarding segregation be answered quickly instead of very slowly, as was being done in Dallas.

There has been a known African American community in Fort Worth since its inception in 1849. Slavery was a larger part of the economy in Fort Worth than in Dallas. And because Fort Worth was an army outpost, many influential officers came to the area. Colonel Middleton Tate Johnson, one of the fort's founding fathers, owned a plantation of 640 acres, and the land was worked by 150 slaves.[56]

After the conclusion of the Civil War, many of the former slaves were removed from plantation work because the yield was no longer profitable. In 1873, the city council hired Hagar Tucker, a former slave, as a special policeman for the black community, but his appointment lasted only a year due to budget cutbacks.[57] Tucker was the first and last black officer in the city until the 1950s.[58]

The first major black businessman, John Pratt, opened a blacksmith shop after Reconstruction.[59] By 1882, the black residents in Fort Worth had developed a full community, including schools, churches and businesses.[60] By 1894, the area had its first black newspaper, *The Item*, which proclaimed itself "The Only Negro Newspaper in the City."[61]

The city of Fort Worth continued to grow, and black and white communities continued to develop next to one another. Even though these communities benefitted from one another, they developed independently.

The Fort Worth race riot of 1913 left the black community at the complete mercy of the white legal system. Homes and businesses were destroyed. The riot was likely a reaction to the economic developments occurring in favor of black laborers. In 1903, a large meatpacking company began hiring black laborers, and in 1907, Texas Steel also began hiring black laborers. In 1937, Riley A. Ransom opened the Ethel Ransom Memorial Hospital, which was designed to serve blacks and was as first-class as any of the local white hospitals.[62]

The size of the black community in Fort Worth helped them to escape most of the overt violence of Reconstruction; however, the small size also made economic development slow. But these resilient residents continued to build up their lives and businesses.

William M. McDonald was Fort Worth's most prominent black businessman in the early 1900s. He eventually grew his wealth through real estate, also owning a pharmacy, a bank and a hotel.[63] He was a leading voice in the community and became an influential member of the Texas Republican Party.

Over time, the black community of Fort Worth grew and represented multiple classes. There were three major neighborhoods for black residents in Fort Worth, and they ranged from poor to wealthy. Another major aspect of the success and resilience of these residents was the birth and thriving nature of large community churches. Even though the legal system and business dealings were largely in the hands of the whites, the church provided a space for all voices to be heard and respected. The New Deal of the 1930s revealed that more than thirty thousand Fort Worth citizens were living in "decrepit, disease-breeding homes."[64] In 1941, the H.H. Butler Fund was established to build newer, better housing. Many of the Butler houses still stand today and are "hemmed in by three freeways and are still a monument to racial segregation."[65] Families braved unwelcoming neighbors when they decided to move into neighborhoods not typically designated for families of a certain race. However, these brave families did just that, and the desegregating of the Fort Worth School District began in 1962.

In 1960, Leonard Brothers broke ranks with the other major business owners and removed his "whites only" and "coloreds only" signs from his department store. By 1963, the downtown stores, restaurants and the theater were all fully integrated. By this time, the police force had black officers, and the *Fort Worth Star Telegram* became the first big-city paper to hire a black reporter. Unlike most of the cities surrounding it, Fort Worth's school integration came in response to public integration instead of preceding it. Since the town was already experienced in integrated life, the school districts integrated without any major reported incidents.

Mansfield, Texas

In 1956, there were only sixty African Americans living in Mansfield, Texas. The elementary schools were segregated, with the non-white school being of far inferior structure. High school–aged students were forced to ride public buses that dropped them off twenty blocks from a school in Fort Worth.[66] Three black students had a suit filed on their behalf by the NAACP, and the city of Mansfield became the first in the state to be ordered to desegregate by a federal court.

That fall, more than one hundred school districts integrated quietly.[67] In Mansfield, however, aided by the mayor and police chief, angry mobs of three to four hundred people protested outside Mansfield High School. They formed a wall of bodies in order to keep the African American students out. The mob burned an effigy of three black people, fistfights broke out on the streets and citizens threatened the sheriff for being an integration sympathizer. Downtown stores closed as a sign of support for the protestors, and vigilantes met people trying to enter the town and turned them away.[68] Governor Shivers called the mob an orderly protest and dispatched the Texas Rangers in order to uphold the segregation of Mansfield schools.

Mansfield, Texas. *Courtesy of Tarrant County College Northeast, Heritage Room.*

Eventually, the angry mob got their way, and the Mansfield school system did not integrate. Mansfield schools eventually did integrate in 1965, when the town consented only after the threat of having its federal funding pulled.[69]

Mansfield is one hour to the southeast of Plano, Texas. It is located to the south of Arlington. Today, one can drive there relatively quickly via toll road, but it is likely that in the 1960s, an individual would have driven south through Dallas proper to get to Mansfield. Many north Dallas high schools still play Mansfield in exhibition football games at the start of their season.

Dallas, Texas

The largest school district in central North Texas is the Dallas Independent School District (DISD). The Dallas school district begins where the Richardson district ends. The distance from Plano's city center to Dallas's city center is only twenty-two miles and a mere twenty-seven minutes. In 1971, a federal judge ordered the integration of the Dallas schools through a busing system similar to those attempted in other cities. Between 1957 and 1971, Dallas claimed compliance with the ruling of *Brown v. Board of Education*, but actions speak louder than words. Although officials claimed that Dallas schools were integrated, many of the people who actually lived in the city told a much different story.

One man who fought this pseudo-integration was named Sam Tasby, who was frustrated that his two sons could not attend the "white school" located near their home.[70] Tasby hired attorney Ed Cloutman in 1970, and they would spend the next thirty-three years pursuing the Tasby case and defending the educational rights of all children.[71] In an interview, Cloutman is quoted as saying, "It was a horrible atmosphere for kids of all colors because it was organized mayhem in schools. It was sort of like, 'You want integration? I'll show you integration.'"[72]

Robert Thomas became a part of the case in 1980 as a lawyer representing the DISD. He expressed that "one of the things that made it difficult was that we had such a large African American population south of Interstate 30 and none north of Interstate 30, which made it very difficult to mix bodies or teachers or anything without crossing the expressway." This was a problem birthed from the historical truth of segregation in neighborhoods. As tensions grew, people were told not to move into the Dalls school district because of the difficulties. And people listened. There was very little immigration of white residents into the DISD for quite some time. And this trend made integration even more difficult, as white students graduated from schools and no new white students entered.

But Dallas is a large city with a large number of schools, and the story wasn't the same for all of them. Student bodies at J.L. Long Middle School and Woodrow Wilson High School were successfully integrated by 1966.[73]

Much like the story in Plano, Woodrow Wilson High School students found their common ground on the football field. A legend at Woodrow Wilson was a young man named John Paul McCrumbly, a 220-pound, six-foot-two junior high student. McCrumbly was fast and strong and had a sweet, endearing personality. He was placed on the varsity team his sophomore year, which was just about unheard of at the time. Then he unwittingly became a uniting factor, somehow making integration easier at the school and more accepted by the students. Naturally, coaches and other players loved him, but his remarkable personality won over everybody else as well.[74]

But not all kids are blessed with athletic talent that can overshadow unfounded stereotypes. At this time, in response to segregation, private schools and church schools became very popular in the city of Dallas. It is now a common sight to see a K-12 school backed by a private church organization. It has become a sort of tradition to have children in private, church-funded schools through their elementary years.

The story of integration isn't only about the students; it also features a vast variety of faculty and administrative staff. In order to combat the rise of church-run private schools, the Dallas Alliance, a task force with the mission of successfully integrating the DISD, started a program of magnet schools. Booker T. Washington High School for the Performing and Visual Arts, the world-famous, arts-focused high school in Dallas, is one shining example of the program's resounding success. The Dallas Alliance worked to create magnet schools with superior standards of excellence. Over time, task force members believed that the schools would become fully integrated on their own because entire communities would not have to be relocated to receive education. Individual students would be admitted based on certain criteria. The plan wasn't fully successful, though, as some residents were willing to sacrifice their children's education in order to validate their dedication to their own convictions.

The appointment of Robert Thomas to the Tasby case in 1980 was the spark that started a fire that would change the landscape in Dallas. Thomas replaced Warren Whitham, a staunch segregationist. When Thomas was put on the case, he met with Whitman, who told him to "fight, fight, fight." But when Thomas called Linus Wright, the Dallas superintendent of schools, to discuss the case, Wright had a totally different opinion.[75] Wright informed Thomas that integration was here and that they had to get it done right. He didn't want to lose students or teachers. Cloutman said he and Thomas became friends because they decided that being friendly served them both more than bickering in a courtroom.[76] The Tasby case was officially dismissed in 2003, thirty-three years after it began.

Keeping Close Watch

Even though there have been many great victories and much progress made over the years, in 2014, there were still nine Texas counties under federal supervision regarding desegregation. Was the fight for equal education a success? Did these educational warriors accomplish their goals? In 1971, the demographics of Dallas were 54 percent white, 36 percent black and 10 percent Hispanic. In 2003, the demographics showed a population that was 6 percent white, 31 percent black and 61 percent Hispanic. When journalist Keri Mitchell asked Thomas and Cloutman whether integration had been achieved, they both said not philosophically or in day-to-day realities, but they believed it had in the eyes of the law, and for them, that was the most important part. That is the real foundation of change for future generations.

Universities

The University of Texas

The University of Texas is one of the largest public universities in the United States. Founded in 1883, it started from a single building with eight teachers.[77] As of 2014, the university has seventeen colleges, twenty-four thousand faculty and more than fifty thousand students.[78] UT now claims to be one of the most diverse universities in the nation. As is true for many southern institutions, the school's mission didn't always extend to include everyone. In 1950, the University of Texas was involved in a major case, *Sweatt v. Painter*, in which the Supreme Court decided that the university's law school and other graduate programs must be opened to African American students since the university could not provide separate but equal facilities.[79] This ruling allowed John Saunders Chase and Horace Lincoln Heath to enroll on June 7, 1950, making them the first two registered African American students at the University of Texas. Their enrollment made UT the first major university in the state to admit both black and white students.[80]

Chase recalled being shadowed by U.S. marshals on campus, receiving hate mail and being on the receiving end of angry slurs. But he also recalled many white students and faculty members accepting him and encouraging him to succeed.[81]

Chase found himself in Texas after taking a job with an architectural firm. When he heard about the outcome of the Herman Sweatt case, he knew he had a chance to attend graduate school and receive his degree in architecture, which would allow him to achieve his dream of designing homes. He appealed to Department of Architecture chairman Hugh Lyon McMath, who advised him to apply to the university and await the outcome.[82] Although admitted, Chase and Heath were not treated the same as other students. Only white students could live on campus or participate in sports programs, and many of the retail shops and restaurants on campus and in the surrounding area were still segregated or refused service to non-whites entirely.

The university made reluctant progress toward integration in its other programs. In 1963–64, Dean Edward Dorn began his freshman year. When Dorn arrived, he was placed in the partly integrated Brackenridge Hall in a section set aside for black students. He recalled that while the campus and surrounding areas were generally open to the African American population, it was always on cautious terms. African American students always knew that some establishments might refuse to serve them.[83] Dorn attributed major changes in Austin race relations to the Civil Rights Act of 1964, believing that when people knew they had rights, they demanded them.[84]

The University of North Texas

The University of North Texas (then known as North Texas State University), located in Denton, had a very successful transition from segregation into integration. The university's president, however, said it was because people did not realize it was happening, not because the area was so progressive.[85] President Matthews worked to keep the news of the university's successful integration quiet in order to continue to protect the students coming into the university.

The University of Texas–El Paso

In 1966, the Texas Western University (now known as the University of Texas–El Paso) Miners became the first team of all-black starters to secure an NCAA national championship. The players drew a lot of ire, and the coach was accused of reverse racism. (Just three years later, in 1969, the University of Texas fielded the last all-white team to win college football's national championship.)

Stephen F. Austin State University

This major university is located in Nacogdoches, Texas, about three hours southeast of the city of Dallas and seven hours northwest of Baton Rouge, Louisiana. In 1958, Ralph Steen was settling into his new position as the president of Stephen F. Austin State University. He immediately began considering integration, as the Herman Sweatt case was often discussed among students and administration. Steen and his mentor, Walter Prescott Webb of the University of Texas, did not consider themselves leaders in race relations. They were simply opposed to segregation and leaders of universities that saw integration as something practical. During a speech Webb made at Steen's integration, he stated that in East Texas, the race issue was "something that, like the pioneer farmer in Texas, who, when he had a log that was too big to move and too green to burn, plowed around it and moved on…If we did nothing but fret about race relations, we would fall behind the rest of the country."[86] With the stage set, Steen was ready to make some strong and contemporarily controversial statements.

One of the larger fraternities on campus complained when it learned that its assigned housing units might be integrated. Steen wrote to them, "You are doubtless correct in believing that Stephen F. Austin will at some time be integrated…We can assign a building to a fraternity, and it will be occupied only by members of that fraternity. The only way in which it could become integrated would be for the fraternity itself to integrate."[87] In this sort of response, Steen was stating that change is here, and if you attempt to stand in the way, you will be run over and left behind.

By 1964, Steen found the integration opportunity that he had been seeking. A young man named Willie Gene Whitaker had been inquiring about how an African American should go about applying to the university, and Steen wrote him back with specific instructions. Steen even told him that he hoped

An anti-Vietnam rally at SFA in 1970. *Courtesy of East Texas Research Center Digital Archives and Collections.*

after the summer board meetings, the application process might be different in that it would be the same for all students.[88] He also encouraged Whitaker to move ahead with the currently in-place segregated application process and told him that he would monitor his application status.

Steen also faced many difficult decisions during his leadership tenure. He was responsible for the denial of two African American students based on the school charter, and he deemed that the community of Nacogdoches was not conditioned the way the students were to accept integration. When schools that were integrated came to play games against Stephen F. Austin, black players had to stay with private families in the area.[89]

Steen had a plan to help the people and students prepare for black classmates. He admitted Reverend Ulysses L. Sanders, an older African American Baptist preacher, for the first summer session of 1964. Steen said that if anyone asked how long Stephen F. Austin had been integrated, everyone was supposed to say "for a while."[90] He believed Sanders would help prepare the community for integration because, in his words, "How could anyone object to an elderly Negro preacher who comes, hat in hand, to get an education?"[91]

Some of the professors left the university in response to integration, and some of the staff resisted. But Steen could not be stopped. He ordered all of the "whites" and "colored" signs to be removed from the university, and when the cafeteria manager refused, Steen went himself, screwdriver in hand, and removed the signs.[92]

Whitaker, who would become the first African American to obtain his degree from Stephen F. Austin State University, had practical reasons for wanting to attend the university far before he had philosophical reasons. The university was closest to his home, his wife and young daughter and his full-time job. Whitaker was seeking a master's degree to benefit his teaching position.[93] He would succeed in his goals and earn his degree in 1966.

Nathaniel West, a Nacogdoches resident, would become the first African American undergraduate to obtain his degree, which he did in 1967. Stephen F. Austin State University welcomed the university's first black athlete in Harvey Rayson, who was recruited to play for the basketball team in 1965.[94] Rayson played a major role on campus after the assassination of Martin Luther King Jr. Even as a young man, he felt that tensions were high, and he realized that if there was not something constructive to do, destructive things would start happening. So he and others unofficially led a memorial to Martin Luther King Jr. that eventually developed into a cultural institution on campus. "Kings Men" became a group dedicated to ensuring equal education and access to all Stephen F. Austin State University students.[95] The group did not last past its inaugural class, but its legacy is still felt. Nacogdoches and Stephen F. Austin State University still work tirelessly to ensure equal education and access to all students.

Texas Tech University

Lubbock, Texas, is known for Buddy Holly and Texas Tech University. The city covers 123 square miles and has a population of about 236,000.[96] Texas Tech is the only school in Texas to house an undergraduate institution, a law school and a medical school at the same location.[97] The university, which opened in 1927, had about 40,000 students in 2014. Texas Tech integrated in 1961 after the threat of a lawsuit following the denial of admission to three African American students. This decision provided the platform for the administration to enact a university policy to admit "all qualified applicants regardless of color."[98] The university embraced this integration in 1967 when it offered its first scholarship to an African American student, Danny Hardaway, who was recruited for the university's football team.

During a later interview, Hardaway stated, "Being the first African American to get a scholarship there…I guess I was kind of anxious initially."[99] Hardaway was the son of an army man, and he knew how to handle being the new kid. "It was also the first time I ever had a white roommate. It was different."[100]

Hardaway recalled that racism was certainly present at that time but that he felt sheltered from it inside the football program and university system. Coach John Conley, who was the school's athletic director from 1980 to 1985, remembered Hardaway being well liked and that when it came to the pressures of being the only black Red Raider, "he handled it very well."[101]

Hardaway was also a disc jockey for the university radio program and would often introduce himself on the air by joking, "Good Morning Lubbock, this is your only black Red Raider." Hardaway remembers liking Lubbock and playing for the Red Raiders. When issues did arise, he would simply "ignore them."[102]

Lubbock had a developed black community at the time of Hardaway's recruitment, and when asked about the city, he said he remembers enjoying the "locals in Lubbock" regardless of race. He said he felt like his teammates and coaches were always out to protect him, and he didn't feel a sense of rejection. "I know a lot of people in Lubbock and West Texas weren't crazy about me being at Tech," he said. "The coaching staff and the other players kind of sheltered me from that. I wasn't naïve…but I couldn't care less. I was there to do a job, get an education and do something I enjoyed."[103] Hardaway also is not naïve about the impact he had on the university and the community in general.

Although Hardaway speaks fondly of his time at Texas Tech, he ultimately spent his senior year at Cameron University after transferring out due to irreconcilable differences with the new head coach, Jim Carlen. But it was not all bad news at Texas Tech; in 1970, Hortense W. Dixon became the first African American to earn his doctorate from the university. Many African American students have made their mark on the world through the research facilities at Texas Tech University, and in 2014, the university boasts a thriving and diverse campus environment.

The University of Houston

The city of Houston is the fourth largest in the United States, hosting 2.6 million people and covering 599.6 square miles.[104] Located on the Texas coast, it is about four hours south of Plano. The University of Houston is the third largest in Texas, with about forty-one thousand students.[105]

The university was originally founded as a private institution in 1927. At first, it was housed at the Old San Jacinto High School, but in 1939, it opened its first two separately constructed buildings.[106] These buildings were located where the school still stands today, in southeast downtown.[107]

In 1963, the school became a state university, and it joined the newly created Houston system in 1977.[108] When the University of Houston was a private institution, it had a segregated "sister school" named Texas Southern University. Phillip G. Hoffman became president of the university in 1961 and oversaw its transition to a state school. He was also the president of the University of Houston when it first began admitting African American

"Wondrous" Warren McVea, the first black athlete for the University of Houston, circa 1969. *Courtesy of Denton Public Library, Denton, Texas.*

students. President Hoffman gathered major players and the press when he decided to integrate. He asked them to allow him to integrate the university quietly. In a 2005 interview, Hoffman recalled, "I told them that we were going to integrate the University of Houston and that we...could either do it quietly or we could have something that resembled Mississippi or Alabama."[109] He wanted the students to be able to simply look around one day and realize that the school had integrated. In reference to to the meeting, he noted that "everyone there agreed that it was best to integrate the university peacefully. So, the university integrated quietly, and that is all there is to it."[110] By 1963, the university had twenty African American students, and in 1964, the football and basketball programs were also integrated. There was a lot of controversy surrounding the silent integration, which was soon being called the "Blackout in Houston."[111] The technique was used all over the city from lunch counters to classrooms.

Across Texas, integration in cities and towns was met with a wide variety of responses. Some experienced a smooth transition; others met with more strife. But over time, integration became a reality for the state. Many indomitable individuals worked with vision and determination to make integration a reality in the classroom, on the athletic fields, at lunch counters on buses and trains and beyond. All of the confusion regarding which schools, coaches and administrators were being progressive and which ones were being oppressive made for some tense interactions and created a breeding ground for suspicion.

Chapter 3

TIME FOR CHANGE

Integration

The high school scene of the 1950s and '60s in Plano in many ways resembled that of today. Musicians, academically minded students, football players, cheerleaders and others filled the halls of schools. But until 1964, all of the students at Plano High School were white.

In 1954, the U.S. Supreme Court case *Brown v. Board of Education* changed the face of education in America by declaring that laws establishing separate public schools for African American and white students were unconstitutional.[112] This ruling, considered a monumental victory for the civil rights movement, set the stage for integration in schools across America. Ten years later, that integration made its way to Plano, Texas.

Following the *Brown v. Board of Education* decision in 1954, the Plano school board discussed the idea of integrating Plano High School with the Plano Colored High School. A citizens committee was formed to discuss the issue, but the consensus was to keep the high schools separate, according to records from 1955 and 1957.[113]

In 1964, the issue came to light again when the school board voted to allow black students of the renamed Frederick Douglass School to decide if they would like to integrate with Plano High School. Students did vote to integrate, making the Frederick Douglass School a facility for primary-level students only. By 1968, the Frederick Douglass School was closed.[114]

"You see, Plano in those days was unique in that everyone raised the kids," said Ken Bangs. "If they saw you out in the community and you needed correcting, they didn't ask Mom and Dad's permission; they corrected you. Plano was truly…it was a village where every member raised the children. I think that there was a foundation already present in the community that made the integration a nonissue."[115]

John Lewis talked about what led to Plano's smooth transition through integration:

> *This is the Douglass community* [Plano's African American community] *just across Fifteenth Street. And the patriarch was Jim Thomas. I'm sure you've heard the stories. He shined shoes forever at Merritt's barber shop. But that was his day job. His real calling was… he had a key ring. He had a key to every commercial building in Plano. If you needed anything done, you would call Jim Thomas…both sides of the tracks. I grew up in Plano about four blocks from here. I knew Jim Thomas as early as I knew anybody. He used to let me hang out with him. I wanted to be a shoe shiner just like he was. He* [taught] *me how to shine black shoes for people wearing white socks and* [how to] *not get any black on their socks.* [He showed me the importance of] *taking pride in that. But as he progressed in age, he would sleep a lot. But he was a patriarch. In Plano, there was a group—and Alton was probably part of this group—in the '50s and '60s that met Wednesday morning* [or] *Thursday morning with Dr. Hendrick, David McCall, Nathan White and Pastor Travis Berry, pastor of the First Baptist Church. They had their own informal leadership program. These were the men in Plano that really were the sounding board and set the direction for where we are today. Jim Thomas was at the table with these people. That was the catalyst. They were city fathers. We all respected them. One of them was my principal and, later, realtor…That set the stage.*[116]

Janis (Frye) Allman graduated from Plano High School in 1961. There were only forty-five students in her class. She recalls that in the summer of 1962, several classmates came up with the idea of a group taking a trip to the Smoky Mountains. They planned a route that would take them through many state capitals and by many college campuses. "We would get off the beaten path, and when we got in that Delta area of Louisiana, Mississippi and Alabama and back off the main roads and back in the cotton fields, it was the most beautiful cotton I had ever seen," she said. "There would be

Wildcat coaches. *Back row, left to right*: Roy Newson, Jack Cockrill and Sherman Millender. *Front row, left to right*: John Clark, Tom Gray and A.J. Brazil. *Courtesy of* The Planonian.

a cutout in the field, and there would be this shack with no electricity, no plumbing, no water...and there would be these black families living there. There were blacks interacting with whites, but there were condescending attitudes. I had never seen anything like that in Plano."[117] In the Deep South, Allman noticed that "whites talked down to blacks" and that "there was an obvious condescending tone the whites used toward the blacks, which is something I never experienced in Plano. Although the neighborhoods we're segregated, we respected our elders, black or white." This concept of a "segregated but civil" community might be what led to easy integration in the school system, she said.[118]

Plano football coach Tom Gray and assistant coach John Clark set the tone for integrating the football team. Player Ken Bangs recalled, "Coach Gray and Coach Clark both were integral in the smooth integration process. [They] valued kids, and they were interested in the community. They didn't brook any nonsense, and if there were issues that kids needed to work out, they let the kids work them out. And if there were issues that they needed to be involved in, they weren't bashful about it. All of the coaches on staff were involved and interested."[119]

Bangs recalled that Plano was somewhat of an enchanted place during that time and that there were certain expectations of everyone. "When we

Wildcat captains. *From left to right*: Jerry Hayes, Ken Bangs and Billy Don Fondren. *Courtesy of* The Planonian.

were growing up in Plano, it was expected that you would do something. You would play in the band, you would do athletics," he said. "If you didn't, Coach Gray called you a 'do-nothing.' We grew up. And I'm telling you, I wanted to be a Wildcat. We grew up with that. When we played, we were playing for Plano."[120]

Bangs also recalled the first time Coach Gray discussed integration with the team: "We did meet. And he did say, 'This is happening' and 'We will be a better team because of it.' And he was right! And that's what I meant when I said they were right up front in dealing with issues. One of Coach Gray's favorite sayings was, 'They put their pants on one leg at a time just like you do.' And he said it. He said, 'These kids are just like you, and we will be a better team with these kids, and I don't expect any problem.' I don't recall him saying specifically that there wouldn't be a problem, but that was just in his personality to make that clear."[121]

Bangs said that the atmosphere in the locker room was "interesting" in the first days following integration:

> *Classroom is one thing. Lunchroom is one thing. When you step into a locker room, it's your world. I can remember the black guys coming in. They didn't know what to expect, and we didn't know what to expect. They stood and looked at us, and we stood and looked at them…and we just came together and started talking. I'm not going to share everything that we said, but we agreed that we were all pretty much alike. Then, in workouts—when we stepped on the field, we worked. Tom Gray ran a no-nonsense program. When you stepped out there for two-a-days, it was quite different. We had black guys with us. And it wasn't just a short time. They were sweating like we were sweating, they were hurting like we were hurting and they were vomiting like we were vomiting. And we came together. If you messed up, it didn't matter. If you did good, it didn't matter. I'm going to tell you, I don't know how we ever lost. We were that blasted good, and we were that together. I was a senior when Kenneth* [Davis] *was a freshman. Coach Gray had gone through the marine corps was a drill sergeant. If he couldn't take you down, he would pull you down. There was no doubt who was the boss, and he did that early…During the integration, after two-a-days especially, you'd all go somewhere and lay out. And there were many times it was just a natural flow, black players and white players laying down together.*[122]

Bangs recalls black and white players riding together on the bus to out-of-town football games. No matter who was on the bus, Coach Gray expected a quiet, respectful atmosphere on the way to games:

> *Everybody was together. We were all on the bus, and we were quiet. If you won, coming home you could get a little bit rowdy. But going, you were quiet. You know what happened? Friends sat with friends. Kenneth Davis and I always sat together. And we kept our eye on* [Johnny] *Griggs. Kenneth Davis was the only superstar we had during my tenure.* [He] *played at the University of Oklahoma. His daddy was a two-time All-American at Texas Southern. He was very quiet. Football was in his blood. He was a leader within the school and a leader on the team. It didn't matter if you were white or black. Kenneth Davis was a leader and, if necessary, an enforcer. He was quiet but very strong and well respected...It was the aura he carried that goes over to you quickly. I was sick with viral meningitis.*

PLANO'S STOUT DEFENSIVE TEAM — Here's one of the state's outstanding 'AA' defensive units, as proved by their record to date. They are: (81) Ronny Davis, (77) Kenneth Davis, (72) Carl Grey, (65) Kent Stout, (74) Neal Olson, (85) Steve Landers, (35) Johnny Pool, (24) Tommy Skelton, (34) Donnie Herrin, (22) Billy Fondren, (53) Kenneth Bangs, (20) Johnny Johnson, (33) Jerry Hayes, (30) Johnny Robinson, (23) Jimmy Merriman and (25) Rodney Haggard.

A *Plano Star Courier* article detailing the amazing defensive team for the Plano Wildcats.

Trudy Turner's cheerleading yearbook photo. *Courtesy of* The Planonian.

When they took me out of isolation and I woke up, sitting beside my bed was Kenneth Davis. If you asked me today to name my top ten friends from high school, Kenneth Davis would be right there.[123]

Bangs echoed a concept shared by many—the idea that football was a uniting force for all residents of the city, no matter their skin color. "The community support and connection went so deep that what you did, you were doing for Plano," he said. "When we put the ball in the air, it was not just a football game. This was Plano. Everyone in Plano was there. They would follow the buses. I remember going to Rockwall to play, and there was nobody in Plano. They were all at the game."[124]

Integration on the field was a time of growth and change for football players in Plano. And integration in the classroom meant new challenges and big learning experiences for students, as well.

"Integration is so obvious in sports—you are forced together," said Trudy (Turner) Bangs, who was a cheerleader at Plano High School from 1964 to 1966 and married football player Ken Bangs. "What was obvious in school is that you were learning to grow together and be together. I remember the first day of integration. I remember being in the classroom. I remember going up to some of the black girls and saying, 'We welcome you to our school.'"[125]

Trudy lived in Dallas but moved to Plano during her sophomore year in high school. She recalled how different race relations were in Dallas:

I saw a lot of things in Dallas. I don't know that here in Plano you had the white bathroom and the colored bathroom that I saw there. I think a lot of it had to do with social skills. It took time for them to feel comfortable with us. [Being] *forced into a locker room together...you're playing a game together. It's just a whole different avenue than sitting in a classroom. We had really great teachers. The trick is, we really didn't have a leader as far as drawing us together. Think about it—in those days...we weren't culturally mature. We didn't have the kind of world view that kids do these days. We didn't have a concept of how we join these two cultures.*[126]

Although the Plano football team and the high school integrated, the cheerleading squad remained all white during those championship seasons. Ken Bangs discussed the difference between competing for a position (football) and being voted for one (cheerleading): "The black girls were

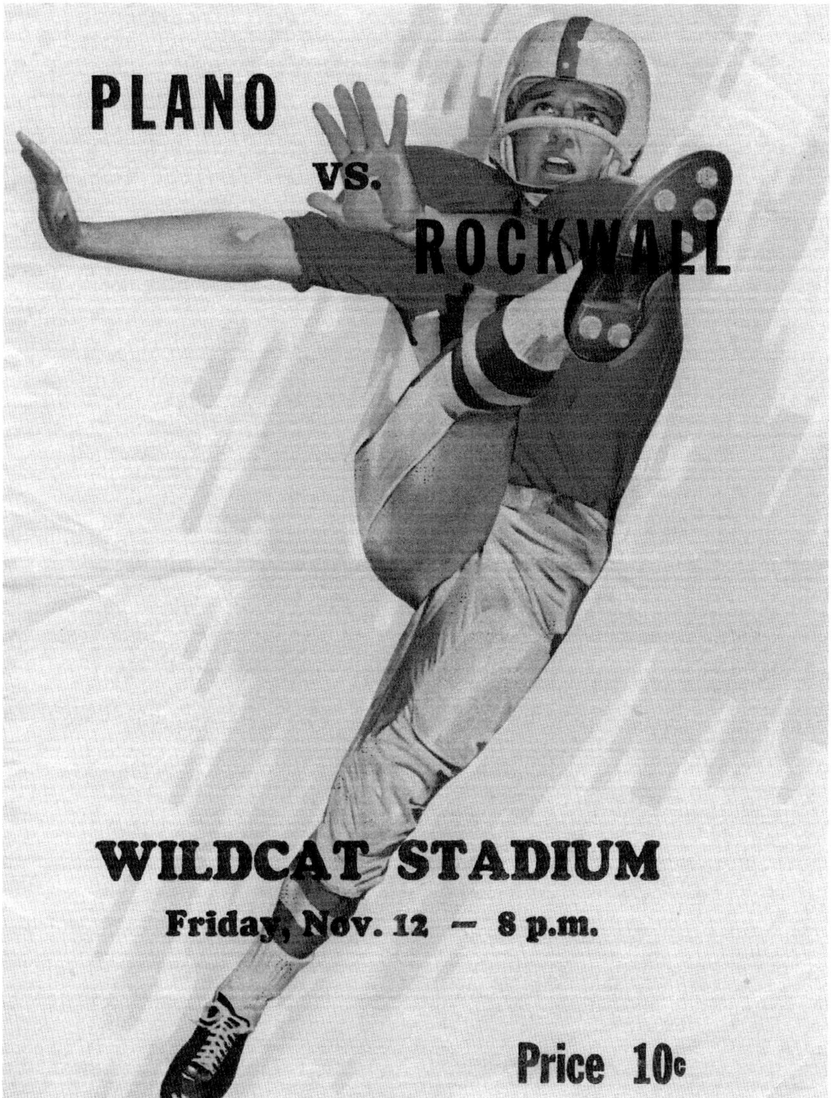

Game program for Plano vs. Rockwall. *Courtesy of the Steve Christie Collection, Haggard Library, Plano, Texas.*

competing against girls that had grown up together and been together from first grade on up. Who are you going to vote for?"[127]

Bangs also added that Plano was not quite ready for progressive actions like interracial dating. "During this period of time, I don't know why, but I got the idea that I wanted to take one of the black girls to the Dairy Queen," he recalled. "Trudy told me I was crazy. Kenneth Davis came to me and said, 'Not a good idea!'"[128]

Former Plano school principal and former mayor Alton Allman remembers some of the other conflicts that came up during Plano's first year of integration: "I had heard that the first year after we integrated that they had a little trouble with the black girls in the high school. And the trouble was that the black boys had such outgoing personalities and flirted with the white girls. Of course, the white girls liked the attention, and the black girls got jealous. There were some cat fights!"[129]

In 1964, Plano desegregated its high school. No one could foresee that the quiet action of this small suburb north of Dallas would be the catalyst that sparked the amazing story of one of the greatest dynasties in the history of Texas high school football.

Voices of Change: Dr. H. Wayne Hendrick and John Freeman Hightower

Dr. H. Wayne Hendrick was elected superintendent of Plano schools in 1961, just prior to a period of rapid growth for the Plano school system.[130] Hendrick was from nearby Lucas, Texas, and had a reputation for being extremely organized, thoughtful and visionary.

"Dr. Hendrick was very instrumental in the smooth integration of the schools," said John Lewis, who played football in Plano from 1960 to 1962, prior to integration.[131]

Alton Allman recalled that Dr. Hendrick had the insight to hire outstanding teachers who not only performed well in the classroom but who were also the right fit for Plano's education system during a time of integration and change. "Dr. Wayne Hendrick had the foresight to hire people like that."[132]

School integration meant integration for both students teachers. Dr. Hendrick worked with Allman to ask several teachers from the Douglass community to join the staff at Plano schools. And many of those teachers became some of the most popular and most requested teachers in the school system. Allman recalls:

> *When we integrated, I went to Dr. Hendrick and requested a teacher from* [the Frederick] *Douglass* [School] *because I knew just about*

> *everybody's reputation down there. So when I requested a teacher,* [Dr. Hendrick] *thought I was real nice to volunteer and do this. I asked for Vivian Haynes. She was a third-grade teacher. I think we had four third-grade classes at that time. We made up a class list for each teacher and put it on the door. Parents came by to see where their kids were going to be. And I had three or four parents come to me, and they didn't want their kids with the black teacher. I said fine and would shuffle them around. But everybody loved that woman—teachers, parents and kids. And by the next year, I had about six people come and say, "Please put my kids in her class."*[133]

Allman recalls that about a week or so before classes started in 1964, Dr. Hendrick ordered school principals and community leaders to "go out in the countryside and find the black people and tell them to come to school."[134] Allman was part of the team that went out to spread the word. "Growing up in Plano and driving by and seeing a little shack sitting out in the field...I didn't think much about it," he said. "But going up to a house and finding people with dirt floors and the raggedy clothes really got to me. We had kids that came to school, first-grade kids, without hardly any clothes or shoes to wear."[135]

But once again, Allman said, the community came together to address problems and challenges. "I've often thought of that many times, and how sad that was that that can be going on in your community and you not even know it. [But] after we all found out about it, we started taking care of those problems."[136]

And it seemed that Dr. Hendrick always knew what was happening in the classrooms, on the football field and behind the scenes. "It surprised me that Wayne Hendrick knew enough things about what was happening on the team and that he cared," said Ken Bangs. "I think he was telling me, 'I know more than you think I know.' He knew what was happening in the hallways, and he knew what was happening on the team. There were a lot of things happening in Plano, and a lot of things that he was the innovator of—team teaching, the open classroom concept, football, athletics. He knew their importance to Plano. He was involved."[137]

John Freeman Hightower came to Plano in 1956 as a science teacher. He was named principal of Frederick Douglass High School in 1964. An important figure in Plano's school segregation, he was not only a strong proponent of integration but also advocated for African American–themed education materials in the classroom.

Hightower, who some affectionately referred to as "the professor," served as a counselor and as director of special services from 1976 to 1984. He

Game program for Lake Worth vs. Plano. *Courtesy of the Steve Christie Collection, Haggard Library, Plano, Texas.*

was later selected as Plano's first coordinator of ethnic relations, a position he held until retiring in 1986. Hightower was named Plano Citizen of the Year in 1978 and also was the first African American to receive the Plano Chamber of Commerce's Outstanding Citizen award. He was a member

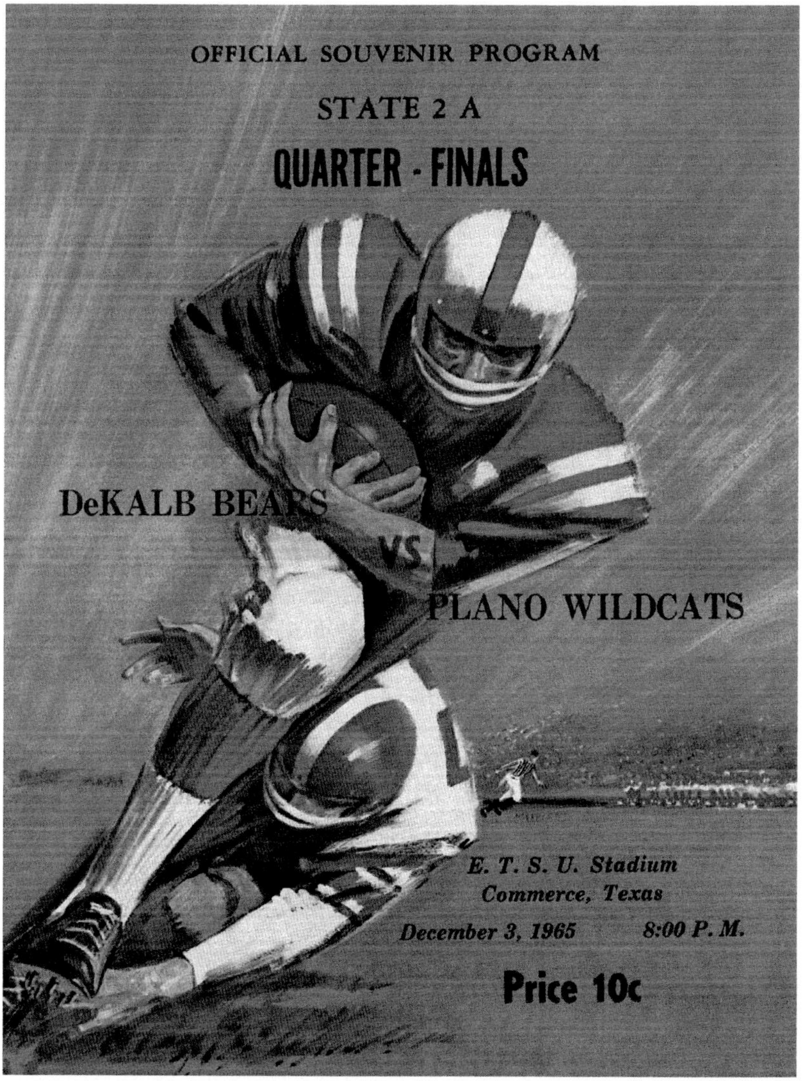

Game program for the DeKalb vs. Plano quarterfinals. *Courtesy of the Steve Christie Collection, Haggard Library, Plano, Texas.*

of the Plano Early Lions Club, which has since named a scholarship in his honor. Hightower Elementary School, named in his honor, opened in the fall of 1998.

"He drove trucks carrying ammunition in World War II," recalled John Lewis of Hightower. "[He] talked about George Patton. As a black soldier, he was carrying live ammunition into active combat, but they wouldn't let him carry a weapon…John was a quiet one. [We called] him "chief" because he had been to the state basketball tournament so many times with the Douglass School."[138]

Integration was a time of many changes, many problems and many possibilities. "When you say 'integration,' the term doesn't fully encompass what happened. It was a polarization of that which had pre-existed," said Ken Bangs. "We were cohesive as a community and as a group of people, and I do believe that Plano was unique. I really do. I heard someone use the term 'Pollyanna,' and maybe that's true in a positive sense. From the outside looking in, someone would have a hard time believing it."[139]

Through the help of great leaders with drive, determination and vision, integration in Plano, both on and off the football field, was a time of great promise. "The community leaders would talk about the needs, and then they would pull the part that they needed to get those needs met," said John Lewis. "There was not a turf war in the community. That was one of the things that made Plano so successful."[140]

Community

As Plano entered the 1960s and the civil rights era, matters of race didn't seem as volatile or ugly as they were in other parts of the country. Janis Allman, a lifelong Plano resident, graduated from Plano High School in 1961, where she played basketball and was a cheerleader. When discussing race relations in Plano, Janis recalls a mutual respect between black and white communities even though they were segregated. "I never looked at Plano and Douglass as being divided," she said. In fact, Janis recalls going to the Douglass community as a child: "We used to go to Douglass and play with the other kids. We always gave the adults respect, and we knew if we misbehaved, it would get back to our parents."

In 1965, players on the newly integrated football team came together pretty quickly. Former player Ronny Hart noted, "I really think that in sports, especially in Plano, the coaches knew their kids. You weren't just meat on the field; the coach knew who you were. If he did not know those kids and was not able to communicate, that wouldn't have worked at all. And most of our coaches are that way even today. There might be eleven different guys on the field, but when they come together, it's one team."[141]

Hart said he often wonders why integration did not happen sooner. "It was such a shame because we had two schools here, and basically we didn't know each other at all," he said. "But when it came time for us to be together, it was, 'This is Plano, and we are going to be Plano and put all of this together.' It was just the cohesiveness of being able to put two groups of kids together into one Plano." He added, "If I think back on it, those of us that were there as kids playing, we had an easier time with it than the adults who were watching. When the kids began to put things together, and the parents saw that it was working, we needed to let it work...I think if there had been a problem with the kids, there would have been a problem everywhere."[142]

But after the 1971 season, the citizens of Plano were seeing only one color: Wildcat maroon. As the victories mounted and the trophy case filled, Wildcat football became the passion of the town and a must-see event in Plano.

Co-founder and co-director of the Plano Conservancy for Historic Preservation, Inc., Russ Kissick, moved to Plano in 1973. Kissick immediately recognized how important football was to the community. "I moved here from Cincinnati. We had major high school [football] programs like Moeller and St. Xavier, but it was nothing like here in Texas," he said. "Football was huge, and it was the only game in town."[143]

Most adults who attend high school football games in America have sons or grandsons on the team. However, in Plano and other Texas towns, the passion for high school football burns a little hotter, according to Kissick: "Everyone went to the games, and everyone had season tickets. It did not matter if you had a son on the team or not." Kissick added that to be a season ticket holder was a big deal in Plano: "I remember the ladies in town would line up to buy season tickets the day they went on sale. They would line up early in the morning before the ticket office opened."[144] "Most everyone also went to the away games," added Kissick. "On Friday nights, when the Wildcats played on the road, Plano looked like a ghost town. Making the playoffs was a given, and everyone looked forward to the playoff games at Texas Stadium [the former home of the Dallas Cowboys in Irving, Texas]. Plano played so many games at Texas Stadium it was like their second home."[145]

Kissick said that following the Wildcats was similar to the way fans follow a professional or major college team. "One year, a group of us chartered an airplane to Midland [West Texas] to see the Wildcats play," he said. "That's how big high school football was in Plano."[146]

Chapter 4
THE COACHES

The Merriam-Webster dictionary defines a coach in three ways:

1) a person who teaches and trains an athlete or performer
2) a person who teaches and trains the members of a sports team and makes decisions about how the team plays during games
3) a private teacher who gives someone lessons in a particular subject

The coaches who have served Plano's Wildcats over the years have not only worked to teach and train the athletes of Plano's schools but have also been instrumental in teaching members of the team about integrity, teamwork, wise decision-making and so much more. These men are legends and have impacted the lives of many.

Tom Gray

1959–65

Coach Tom Gray, who led Plano's first integrated team to a state championship, was born on February 6, 1930, in San Angelo, Texas. Coach Gray played football at San Angelo Junior College (now Angelo

State University) and North Texas State University. As a college football player, he went by the nickname "Potty" because his five-foot-seven-, 180-pound body resembled a pot.[147] After college, he served his country as a first lieutenant and ammunition specialist in the U.S. Marines during the Korean War.

His first high school head coaching job was in McKinney, Texas, leading the McKinney Lions. He coached the Lions for four years and then accepted both the athletic director and head football coach positions at Plano High School in 1959. The Plano football dynasty started with Coach Gray, as the two Plano coaches before him each had losing records. Coach Gray made two significant changes that turned Plano's football fortunes. The first was installing the "Wing-T" offensive formation, and the second was developing a football program for the seventh- and eighth-grade athletes.

1962
FOOTBALL SCHEDULE
PLANO WILDCATS

Sept. 7—Lake Highland there.
Sept. 14—Duncanville there.
Sept. 21—Seagoville here.
Sept. 28—Bonham here.
Oct. 5—Lancaster there.
Oct. 12—Open date.
*Oct. 19—Rockwall here.
*Oct. 26—Cooper there.
*Nov. 2—Whitesboro here
*Nov. 9—Commerce here.
*Nov. 16—Lewisville there.
* Denotes conference game

—Compliments—
PLANO FUTURE
FARMER CHAPTER

A game schedule to be kept in your wallet or purse. *Courtesy of the Steve Christie Collection, Haggard Library, Plano, Texas.*

Coach Gray's hard work and planning would pay off in 1961 as the Wildcats achieved an undefeated regular season. "Our senior year [1961], we were undefeated until losing to Jacksboro [20–12] in the regional playoffs," said Owen Haggard, who was inducted into the Plano Independent School District Hall of Honor in 2014. "That was Tom Gray's third year at Plano. We had not done well the few years before he came to Plano. Coach Gray started the winning tradition that Plano still enjoys today."[148]

More changes were in store for Coach Gray and the Plano Wildcats in 1964. The new home of the Wildcats, Williams Field, opened. Coach John Clark joined the athletic department as a basketball coach and junior varsity football coach. Coach Gray

A 1965 team photo (taken before Johnny Griggs was moved up from junior varsity) that was featured on the back of that season's game programs. *Courtesy of the Steve Christie Collection, Haggard Library, Plano, Texas.*

Wildcat football captains Randall Chaddick and John Griggs. *Courtesy of* The Planonian.

also changed the offense from the "Wing-T" to the "I-Slot."[149] However, the biggest change was all-white Plano High School integrating with Frederick Douglass High School.

Although integration went more smoothly in Plano than in some other areas of the state, there were still bumps in the road. Coach Clark said, "The acceptance went out to the community from the school. The young people that came together for the program and for the school did very well. It took a while for our fans to say, 'This is our team.'"[150]

In 1965, Coach Gray and the newly integrated Plano Wildcats would achieve something no other Plano football team had accomplished. On December 18, in rainy Austin, Texas, the Wildcats defeated the Edna Cowboys to claim the school's first state championship. Coach Gray would leave Plano after winning the state championship. He would coach Palo Duro in 1966 and Irving in 1967 before finally putting down roots at Mesquite High School, where he would lead the Skeeters from 1968 to 1977.

When Coach Gray took over in 1968, the Mesquite Skeeters football team had not made the playoffs since 1941. Coach Gray slowly built the program, just as he did in Plano. The hard work would pay off in the magical year of 1974.

In the *Mesquite News*, Devin Hasson recalled the powerful Skeeters of 1974:

> *The drought finally ended in 1974, and Mesquite made the most of just its second playoff appearance in school history. Under Coach Tom Gray, the Skeeters did not lose a game in racing to an 8-0-2 record in the regular season and the District 8-4A championship. Mesquite earned its first playoff victory with a 20–13 win against Irving MacArthur and did not stop there. The Skeeters defeated Wichita Falls Rider, 14–0, and then after their game with Amarillo Palo Duro ended in a 10–10 tie, advanced on penetrations. In the state semifinals, Mesquite knocked off Carter, 14–12, to advance to the Class 4A state championship game, where they fell just short against Brazoswood in a 22–12 loss to end the season with an 11-1-3 record.*[151]

To make it the state championship, Mesquite had to overcome not only a quality opponent but also the weather. The state semifinal was played in a dense fog. Coach Gray said at the time that he didn't even see the game-clinching interception: "I heard the crowd roar, and how they saw it, I'll never know."[152] For his efforts, Coach Gray was named Texas High School Coach of the Year.

Coach Gray also served as the director of the High School Coaches Association from 1965 to 1967. In 2006, he was inducted into the Plano Independent School District Athletic Hall of Honor. Coach Gray passed away on July 17, 2012. He is fondly remembered by his contemporaries.

"Tom ran a tight ship and got young men to play hard for him," said Coach John Clark. "If you have those two things, you are going to be just fine. Tom set up a good foundation here at Plano, and I obviously benefited from that."[153]

"That title in '65 was huge," said Tom Kimbrough, former Plano head coach who took over in 1976. "Coach Gray set the winning tradition in terms

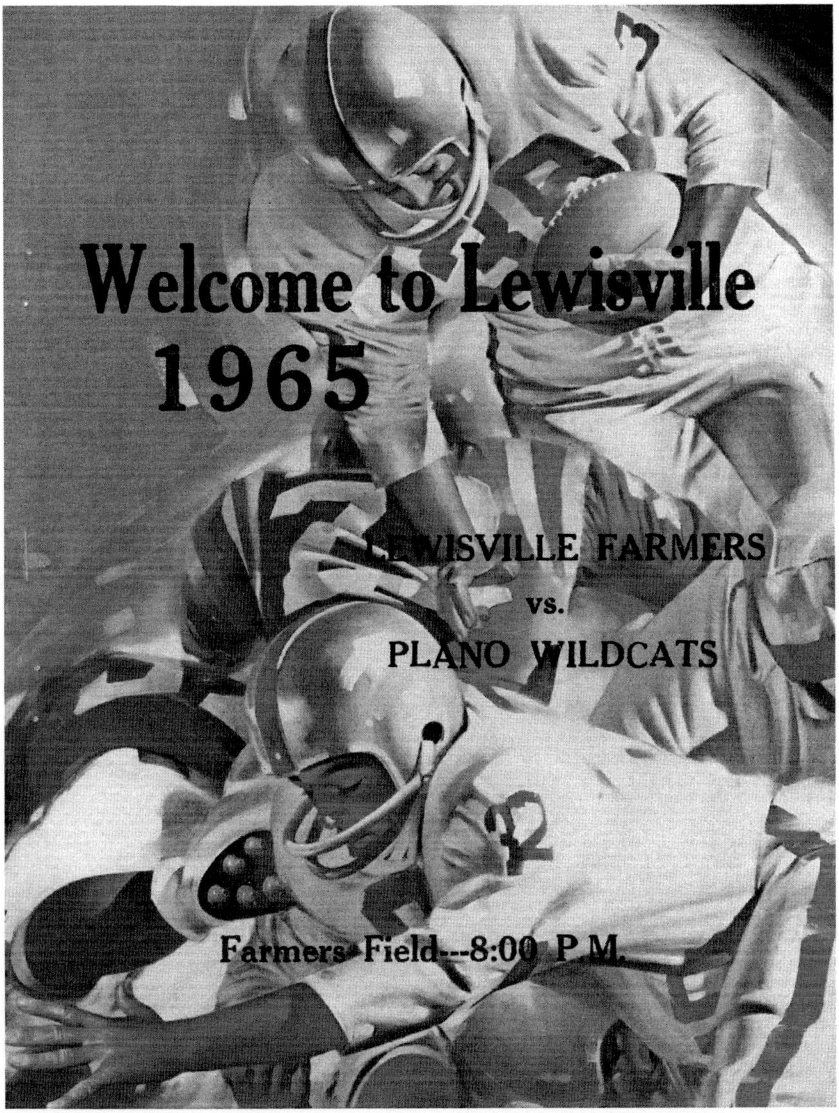

Game program for Lewisville vs. Plano. *Courtesy of the Steve Christie Collection, Haggard Library, Plano, Texas.*

of state championships. And once you establish that tradition, it's a lot easier to fill the program and sell the community on what you are doing."[154]

"Coach Gray impacted countless lives during his years at Mesquite High School," said Steve Bragg, McKinney Independent School District athletic director. "There are a lot of people still tied to the school district—employees,

NOW STANDS THE FIRST SIGN on the outskirts of Plano, advertising the home of the new State AA Football Champions. Located near Griffin Oldsmobile on Central Expressway, the maroon and white sign is the courtesy of A. R. Schell, Jr. and W. E. (Pete) Ford. Motorists traveling North can view this latest erection denoting the Wildcat honors.

The first sign constructed to honor the Wildcat state champions. *Courtesy of the* Plano Star Courier.

ex-employees, former players and coaches—who got their start through him and worked with him. And they all have shared fond memories. He touched a lot of lives and had a huge impact on MISD."[155]

Coach Gray's influence is also reflected in his players. Even after a half century, the effect he has had on their lives is obvious. Two of his players, Ken Bangs and John Lewis, discuss the imprint Coach Gray left on them. "I have to tell you I loved the man," said Bangs. "Tom Gray was the one who turned Plano football around." Bangs added:

> *Coach Gray believed that you needed to reach beyond yourself to achieve as much as you could. That stretching is what caused the growth. We were a 2A team, but we played a lot of 3A teams. The UIL would let you go one classification above. All of our pre-district games were 3A teams, and we blew them out. We just massacred them. We won because we were the best prepared, not because we were great athletes. We didn't have a superstar on*

the team until we integrated, but we were so well prepared...because of Tom Gray and his system. John Clark is a great coach, and I love him, too. Tom Gray deserves more credit than he gets. When John Clark came, they were just awesome together. They had us totally prepared for every game. That was the difference. Coach Gray used to tell us that if someone comes to Plano and there's a spitting contest, they'd better bring two buckets of

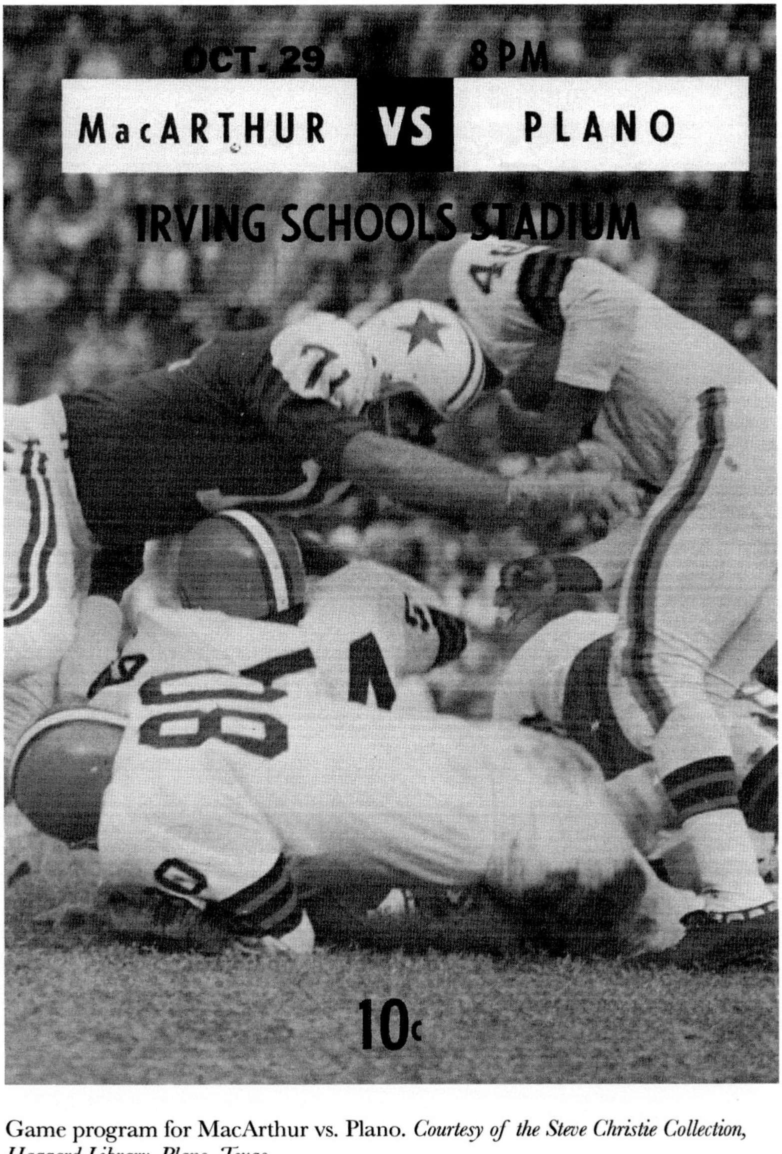

Game program for MacArthur vs. Plano. *Courtesy of the Steve Christie Collection, Haggard Library, Plano, Texas.*

water. When our team was inducted into the Hall of Fame, Coach Gray was there of course. I got a chance to talk to him...I grew up without a dad. He was my dad.[156]

John Lewis said:

He changed my life. And it was thirty years later that I wrote him a letter thanking him. Coach Gray came down in fall of 1959. He had been coaching in McKinney. He said, "No nonsense." He was probably the best-educated classroom teacher I had. There was no room for error, for not caring. We went 0-10 for the two years before he came. He said, "If you will be dumb enough to follow me and do what I tell you, I will make winners out of you." The first year, we were 5-5, the next year 6-2-2 and the third year 10-0.

Coach Gray was a pain in the butt. If you believed in him, he would do wonderful things. He changed boys into men. He knew what you were doing 24-7. I thought I knew Coach Gray. He has a life so far beyond what we did together. If you couldn't keep your mouth shut and if you couldn't do your job, Coach Gray didn't have a use for you. Chicken [one of the football players without great athletic skills] *was one of his boys. You didn't have to be a good player for Coach Gray to support you. Stubby Warden came into Ranger* [Texas], *and the entire community coalesced into one body that would move.* [Stubby Warden was the coach at Ranger High School and winner of the 1953 state championship.] *And Coach Gray did that.*

Coach Gray set the foundation. He hired John Clark. Coach Gray taught you how to be a man. We had guys who came out every year and wanted to play football, but they couldn't survive the two-a-days. They wanted to play, but they weren't willing to sacrifice. Coach Gray knew that if you couldn't do that, you wouldn't be there for the fourth quarter. One thing that I did—I worked and worked. He knew that, and he appreciated that. He called me into his office and said, "I am going to do something that I have never done before." He said, "I am going to appoint you one of the three football captains." He had the confidence in me. He planted that seed early. Those seeds were planted very deeply, and they were fertilized, watered and cultivated in Plano. A lot of that still carries on today.

I was at North Texas [University of North Texas] *going back and forth to TI* [Texas Instruments]. *Coach Gray quit a year or so later...he took a job at Amarillo* [Palo Duro] *High School because it was a 4A*

—Dallas News Staff Photo.

The Road to State Title

Cheerleader Sally Jones points out the mission to Plano coach Tom Gray and three of his Wildcat players who will seek the state AA high school football championship Saturday. The Wildcats meet Edna at Austin at 7:30 p.m. for the title. The Players, from left, are Johnny Griggs, Bill Fondren and Johnny Robinson. It's the first state title game for Plano.

Coaches and players featured in the *Plano Star Courier*.

school. He goes up there and lasts one year and quits and comes to Irving. I hadn't seen Coach Gray in two or three years. One Friday night, I came in early, and I went to Irving to see a football game coached by Coach Gray. When the game was over, I went by the fence as the men were coming off the field. Coach Gray came over, and he loved on me and hugged me. I didn't hold myself out to be worthy of that type of attention.

Coach Gray is a team player. He came back and talked to me, and he talked about how good it was to see us. He said, "I gave up the best job in the world. I thought I could do better and sffect more people." He said, "Y'all were the most coachable bunch of guys, and your parents were the most participating parents without being overruling and over burdening." If we meant that to him, he meant that much to us in spades.[157]

John Clark

1966–75

After two years as a Plano assistant coach, John Clark took over the head coaching duties in 1966. Coach Gray had left after the 1965 state championship season to take the head coaching job at Amarillo's Palo Duro High School.

"He asked if I wanted to come with him to Amarillo," Clark said. "I told him, 'No Tom, I believe I'll stay here and see if I am lucky enough to get the Plano job.'"[158] However, it almost did not happen. Coach Clark

Coaches after John Clark became head coach. *From back left to front right*: Keith Sockwell, Harold Mayo, Robert Woodruff, Jake Swann, Larry Guinn, John Clark and Sherman Millender. *Courtesy of* The Planonian.

Entrance to the Tomato Bowl in Jacksonville, Texas, where Coach Clark was born and raised and where he played football. *Courtesy of Jeff Campbell.*

eventually resigned and accepted a position at Henderson High School in the Piney Woods of East Texas. The school board met in a special session on a Monday night and convinced Clark to stay. In addition to accepting the head coaching position, Coach Clark took on the role of athletic director.[159]

John Clark was born on January 10, 1934, in the East Texas town of Jacksonville. As a youth, Clark was an all-round athlete, playing both offense and defense on the football team. He also played basketball, baseball and tennis. He played basketball at Lon Morris Junior College and received his bachelor's degree from Baylor University.

After college, Clark started his teaching and coaching career at Amarillo High School in 1957. At Amarillo High School, he served as an assistant to the Houston Oiler's legendary Coach Bum Phillips in 1959. After Amarillo, he coached and taught at Weatherford and his home town of Jacksonville before arriving at Plano in 1964.

Many people credit Coach Clark for welcoming the African American football players from Douglass High into the Plano program during desegreation. Coach Clark said, "I don't think I had a part in it. I can remember one or two who got discouraged and thought about dropping out. I told them that it would be the first time we had someone from Douglass quit. It wasn't me; it was the players themselves. They expected a lot out of one another. My job was easy."[160] James Thomas, who played for Coach Clark after transferring from Douglass, recalled, "In our neighborhood…we knew Coach Clark, and we were taught to trust and believe in him."[161]

Thomas recalled that in many ways, integration in Plano seemed like a simple process, even though the behind-the-scenes story was likely very different:

> *It seemed like that transition was so seamless. I know there were a lot of things done behind closed doors and all. My dad was involved in NAACP scenarios going on in Dallas. They communicated with some of the Plano representatives. As far as making that transition…it was well communicated. My parents, and my dad especially, learned an awful lot about what was going on and were well educated. They made it work. It was very amicable. We knew that we had a Caucasian society. We were not aware that it was so different from ours. Behind closed doors, it may not have been that way. But for us, it wasn't that difficult at all.*[162]

In the ten seasons Clark served as the Wildcats' head coach, Plano won two state championships and nine district championships. Coach Clark would compile an amazing record of 107-17. It was fitting that the Baylor graduate's first state championship, a 27–8 victory over San Antonio Randolph in 1967, was clinched at Baylor Stadium in Waco. The day after winning state, Coach Clark taught his Sunday school class.[163] In 1971, he won his second state championship, a close, hard-fought 21–20 triumph over Gregory-Portland in a game played at the Memorial Stadium on the University of Texas campus in Austin. Coach Clark also led Plano to two undefeated regular seasons in 1974 and 1975. The Wildcats lost in the 1974 state quarterfinals to Dallas Carter and in the 1975 bi-district to Longview.

After relinquishing his head coaching duties, Coach Clark would serve Plano Independent School District as athletic director for the next seventeen years. In 1977, the Plano Wildcats would play their inaugural season at John Clark Field. The Wildcats really knew how to open a new stadium, as they would finish the season with the school's fourth state championship. It would be one of three state championships under Coach Clark's leadership as athletic director.

Coach Clark would become the first inductee into the Plano Athletics Hall of Honor. He is also a member of the Texas High School Coaches Association Hall of Honor, the Texas High School Athletic Directors' Hall of Honor and the Texas Sports High School Football Hall of Fame.

"John Clark was very inspirational and was my role model," said Coach Tom Kimbrough. "Any success I had, I share with him because he taught me everything I know. He was so instrumental in whatever success I've had over the years."[164]

Actor Brad Leland Williams, one of the stars of the television show *Friday Night Lights*, played football for Coach Clark and the Plano Wildcats but suffered a devastating knee injury. "I stood there, crying my eyes out," recalled Williams. "I told Coach Clark, 'I know my knee's done.' It was the hardest

COACH JOHN CLARK is the author of an article appearing in "The Texas Coach," a magazine distributed widely among professional sportsmen in Texas.

Star 11-17-65

"Texas Coach" Features Article By John Clark

The October issue of "The Texas Coach" contains a two-page basketball article entitled "Last Minute Play" by John Clark, basketball coach at Plano High School.

The editors of the magazine asked Clark to write an article to interest and inform other coaches on some subject pertaining to basketball, and Clark chose to write about the crucial periods of play during the game.

Along with the article in the magazine, which isdistributed magazine, which is distributed widely throughout the state, appears a picture of the Plano coach and several diagrams of basketball plays.

During the fall, Clark's time is filled with football since he also serves as assistant football coach, but he confessed that basketball is his favorite sport.

His interest in baseketball was encouraged last year by his local cagers advancing to the regional play-off.

Sports became more than a hobby for Clark at Jacksonville High School, Jacksonville, Texas, where he lettered in all the major events, and athletic activities continued to occupy most of his time later at Baylor University where he majored in physical education and lettered in basketball.

While serving as a professional coach and teacher, he has taught at Amarillo, Weatherford and Jacksonville before joining the faculty at Plano.

Clark's enthusiasm for sports is also shared by his wife, 8-year-old daughter Janet and 6-year-old Susan.

In addition to his local coaching duties, he teaches eighth grade science and boys' physical education.

Coach John Clark wrote and published an article entitled "The Texas Coach." Pictured is the *Plano Star Courier* honoring his publication.

From left to right: Randall Chaddick, James Thomas, Ronny Hart and Coach John Clark. *Courtesy of Kirby Stokes.*

thing I'd ever done. I'd never quit anything in my life. But the coach said, 'Brad, you're a good actor. You go and pursue that. But if you ever feel like you're ready to go, your locker is always there. You know you love acting—go get it, son.'"[165]

Former player Ronny Hart recalled, "Coach Clark made everything roll. He was able to bring out the best in you. He expected the best in you. Everybody respects Coach Clark!"[166]

Ken Bangs added, "When we were seniors, John was the assistant. He was a great coach, he cared about the kids and he was organized. The thing about John with black players is...There was a kid by the name of Alex Williams who was QB [quarterback]. The competition was really strong that year between Alex and a white kid. John showed up. There was a lot of conflict about that. John said, 'I'm playing the best athlete.'"[167]

"Coach Clark had to have the courage to say 'I am playing this athlete,'" recalled John Lewis. "John Clark wanted to win. But he did what was right for the team and the athletes. When he said, "I am playing this kid," it was because that kid deserved to play."[168]

Tom Kimbrough

1968–75 (Assistant Coach) and 1976–91 (Head Coach)

Tom Kimbrough was born on October 25, 1944, in Hamilton, Texas. His high school years were spent in Valley Mills, Texas, where he played for Coach A.E. Drew. A graduate of Texas Christian University, Coach Kimbrough is a member of the Texas Christian University Alumni Hall of Fame and a 1988 recipient of the university's Frog O'Fame Award, which is given to alumnus who have achieved recognition through their career in the field of sports. While still attending Texas Christian University, he scouted games for Plano High School in 1967. Coach Kimbrough joined the Plano football staff as an assistant coach under Coach John Clark in 1968.

"Plano and Tom Kimbrough were a perfect fit when he got a job there as assistant coach in 1968. He was a humble, unassuming guy from tiny Valley Mills. Plano was a country town that had just won its second Class 2A state title. The city would change drastically over the next two decades as it morphed from a small farming town into a burgeoning Dallas suburb. Yet, somehow, Kimbrough remained a perfect fit."[169]

Kimbrough would serve as an assistant coach to Coach John Clark's Wildcat football dynasty until 1975. When Coach Clark decided to hang up his coaching whistle after the 1975 season, Kimbrough became the team's head coach.

In sixteen years as Plano's head coach, Tom Kimbrough would win three state championships (1977, 1986 and 1987). In 1978, the Wildcats would make another appearance in the state title game, losing 29–13 to one of the greatest teams in Texas high school football history, Houston Stratford. Plano would also achieve four undefeated regular seasons under Coach Kimbrough's tenure (1982, 1983, 1984 and 1987). Coach Kimbrough's Wildcats hold one of the longest Texas high school winning streaks, a twenty-nine-game run that lasted from October 3, 1986, to September 9, 1988.

Coach Kimbrough was one of only four high school coaches honored on *Dave Campbell's Texas Football*'s list of the top ten most memorable Texas football coaches. "Kimbrough never changed what he stood for in his 16-year head coaching career: a strong work ethic, organization and discipline. Plano was a quintessential powerhouse program, churning out talented players and disciplined teams year after year. There was nothing flashy about the Wildcats or Kimbrough, except for the shiny trophies they claimed at the end of the year."[170] The list is quite an honor when you consider

Part of the display in the front entrance of the Clark Stadium offices. *Courtesy of Kirby Stokes.*

that it includes the Dallas Cowboys' Tom Landry and the Texas Longhorns' Darrell Royal.

Kimbrough's overall record in sixteen seasons was a stellar 171-28-7, and he was named Texas High School Coach of the Year three times (1977, 1986 and 1987). Also, in 1987, Kimbrough was named National High School Coach of the Year, and in 1983, he garnered the *Dallas Morning News*' SportsDay High School Coach of the Year award.

After his coaching career, Kimbrough served the Plano Independent School District for ten years as athletic director. In those ten years, he directed more than twenty-one athletic teams to state championship games, twelve of which emerged victorious. Like Coach John Clark, Tom Kimbrough would have a stadium named for him. Tom Kimbrough Stadium opened in 2004 and has a capacity of 9,800.

Billy Ray Smith, former Plano Wildcat, University of Arkansas All-American and San Diego Charger All-Pro, recalled, "There's no doubt the reason I'm a professional football player is because of the instruction from Coach Kimbrough and the other coaches. He was a coach who believed in preparation down to the smallest detail."[171]

Gerald Brence, current Plano Independent School District athletic director and former Plano High School head football coach, who served as an assistant coach under Kimbrough, added, "Coach Kimbrough is totally committed to his faith, his family and then to his team. He is a tremendous motivator and teacher. His greatest attribute is bringing it all together. Kids took away much, much more than football in his program. They took away what we're all about in Plano athletics: character, academics and then athletics. Everybody who coached or played with Kimbrough remembers this process."[172]

Jason Duvall, a former offensive tackle who played under Coach Kimbrough, said, "He likes everybody to be the same, to be one. He wants forty-six guys to be one. He does an excellent job at that. He has been a winner; we follow, and it works."[173]

Weldon Leon "Jake" Swann

1965–69 (Assistant Coach)

Weldon Leon "Jake" Swann was born on May 8, 1935, in Jacksboro, Texas. He attended Texas Tech University, where he was a baseball standout for the Red Raiders. After college, his football coaching career would take him to Robstown, Sherman and then Plano.

From 1965 to 1969, Swann was an assistant coach with the Plano Wildcats, first serving under Coach Gray and then Coach Clark. After 1969, he left for Bonham, Texas, where he served as an assistant in 1970 and then took over the head coaching duties in 1971. Coach Swann would remain at Bonham until 1977, when he went on to coach at Mesquite from 1978 to 1980. However, he would return to Plano after the 1980 season.

In the late 1970s, Plano, Texas, and Collin County were growing at an accelerated rate. Due to the population boom, the Plano Independent School District made the decision to establish a new high school, Plano East Senior High School. Coach John Clark recommended Coach Swann to lead the upstart Plano East Panthers program.[174] In 1981, the Panthers would play a junior varsity schedule, holding off on a varsity schedule until the following year.

Coach Swann's most rewarding game had to be against the rival Plano Wildcats in 1982. Trailing 14–7 late in the game, the Panthers scored a touchdown to cut the lead to one point. Coach Swann did not want to go for the tie and instead opted to go for the win. The two-point conversion came up inches short of the goal line, and the Wildcats were able to hold off their newest rival by the score of 14–13. It must have given Coach Swann and his Panthers satisfaction to take their neighbors, a perennial Texas powerhouse, down to the wire.

Coach Swann would lead the fledgling Panthers to back-to-back 4-6 seasons in 1982 and 1983. The 1983 season would be Swann's last coaching in Plano. It is always a challenge to start a football program from scratch. The coaches who start these programs know the challenges that lay before them. Although Coach Swann was at Plano East for only two years, he laid the cornerstone of a program that would win six district championships from 1985 to 2000.

After his stint with the Plano Wildcats as an assistant, winning two state championships and starting a new football program at Plano East, Coach Swann will always be a part of Plano football lore.

The Merriam-Webster dictionary's third definition of a coach is someone who "gives someone lessons in a particular subject." For the Plano Wildcats, the coaches have certainly taught not only offense, defense, passes, plays and teamwork but also the life lessons of acceptance, kindness, determination, hard work and compassion, which are perhaps even more important. The Plano Wildcats had the opportunity to learn all of those lessons simultaneously from great men who were committed to their team, their school, their community and to making a difference in Plano and beyond.

Chapter 5

THE STADIUMS

Football can be played in a soggy, muddy field or a dazzling state-of-the-art stadium under the Friday night lights. Fans will gather to cheer their team to victory whether huddled along the sidelines in the sleet and rain or seated in shiny new bleachers. Plano's Wildcats have played ball in a variety of settings over the years, including everything from a cow pasture to a jaw-dropping professional football stadium. No matter the setting, one thing remains the same: Plano loves this game.

Rice Field

Circa 1925–63

A group of boys formed an unsanctioned Plano football team in 1898. In 1900, the first official high school team was formed. By 1914, Plano had not only a football team but also men's and women's basketball teams. But as World War II began, all athletics were temporarily cancelled. There were simply not enough men to field any teams.[175]

By 1925, however, athletics programs in Plano had been reestablished and a mascot chosen: the Wildcat. That same year, the football team completed an undefeated season. The resulting fervor led to increased funding of athletics in Plano. The district allocated funds to purchase a cow pasture for the purpose of playing football and other sports. The pasture was renamed Rice Field after two men who played key roles in the team's history.[176]

Joe Rice was a Plano school board member until 1930 and also farmed in the area. In fact, his mules did most of the field grading by pulling fresno scrapers across the lot. His brother, Guy M. Rice, was manager of the original Plano football team in 1900, when Joe played on the team. Guy served on the school board from 1917 to 1919, and Joe served from 1922 to 1930 and from 1933 to 1935.[177]

The field that started off as a cow pasture had some issues. The south end of the field was lower than the north end. Those visiting for the earliest games at the field had no formal seating. Fans stood along the sidelines or watched games from their cars in inclement weather.[178]

John Lewis played football in Plano prior to the city's school integration. He recalls much time spent at Rice Field: "Dale and Peanut were great football players. They'd play on Saturday night. We'd play on Friday night. I guarantee you that where the bus barn was at the end of Rice Field—our home football stadium—many of the black community would be down there watching our ball games. And on Saturday night, I'd go watch them play. I don't know what that proves, but we always had a good relationship with each other."[179]

Over time, improvements and changes came to Rice Field. Lights were installed at the field before the 1934 season, put in by the football players themselves. The field was also used for Plano's black high school football teams from about 1931 on.[180]

By 1939, the Rice Field boasted many more amenities, including seats for one thousand spectators, flushing toilets installed at the northwest corner of the field and a small press box. At that time, the field was rimmed by barbed-wire fencing and gravel paving. Admission to games was about thirty-five to forty cents.[181]

But the glory days for Rice Field were short-lived. With the construction of Plano High School (which is today known as T.H. Williams High School) in 1957, an accompanying stadium was built, and Rice Field was abandoned. Rice Field has since been demolished.[182]

Williams Field/Wildcat Stadium

1964–76

A landmark in the Plano Independent School District, T.H. Williams High School (originally named Plano High School) was constructed on Seventeenth Street in 1961 at a cost of $993,590. In its first year, the school included grades eight through twelve, and the total enrollment was 390 students. Enrollment grew steadily until the 1965–66 school year, when it suddenly dropped to 653. The following year, the school stopped hosting eighth-grade students, and enrollment fell to 555. Two years later, it became a grade ten through twelve facility with 627 students. A new senior high school was completed in 1975, leaving the Williams campus with 938 freshmen and sophomores.[183]

When the new Plano Senior High School opened in 1975, the Plano High School was renamed in honor of Thomas Howard "Bill" Williams (1902–1992), a beloved teacher, coach and principal who gave almost five decades of service to educating youths of Collin County.[184] Williams had come to the district in 1936 as a math instructor and also served as head football coach from 1943 to 1953, leading his teams to several district and state titles.

The Plano School Board purchased the land for Williams Field for $1,000 per acre in the 1950's from the Forman estate. The purchase was controversial at the time because many in town thought the price was too high. The stadium opened in 1964, with west-side seating reserved for the "home" crowd and east-side seating designated for overflow and general admission. Stands from the east side of Rice Field were taken to Williams Field for temporary use until new stands could be constructed. The seating capacity was eventually expanded to eight thousand.[185]

John Clark Field/Stadium and Tom Kimbrough Stadium

1977–Present

The Plano Wildcats now play home games at two stadiums: John Clark Stadium and Tom Kimbrough Stadium. John Clark Field opened in 1977 and underwent renovations from 2003 to 2007. When renovations were

North Texas football spectators, 1995. *Courtesy of University of North Texas Archives.*

completed, the facility was renamed John Clark Stadium. It was named for Coach John Clark, who led the Wildcats to state titles in 1967 and 1971.

Plano completed initial construction on John Clark Stadium at a cost of $2.75 million. The stadium, with a capacity of 14,224, is the facility used for most varsity football games today. John Clark Stadium is a multi-use stadium that is used for high school football and soccer. The stadium is owned by the Plano Independent School District and is the home stadium of Plano Senior High School, Plano West Senior High School and Plano East Senior High School.[186]

Completed in 2004, Tom Kimbrough Stadium, which is located in Murphy, Texas, is the other home field for Plano's teams. It is named in honor of Coach Tom Kimbrough, who won three state titles and a national title and also served as athletics director.

Texas Stadium: Playing Like the Pros

1979

The Plano Wildcats played part of the 1979 season at Texas Stadium, formerly the home of the Dallas Cowboys. In fact, the Plano team played more games at Texas Stadium than any team other than the Dallas Cowboys.[187]

Texas Stadium was almost like another home field for the Plano Wildcats football team. Coach Kimbrough recalled that "being the home team at Texas Stadium really has no impact other than choosing the side of the field to control the traffic flow."[188]

Whether it is played in a muddy field or shiny new stadium, football means a lot to the people of Plano. Players of every color, income level and educational background come together on the field as a team.

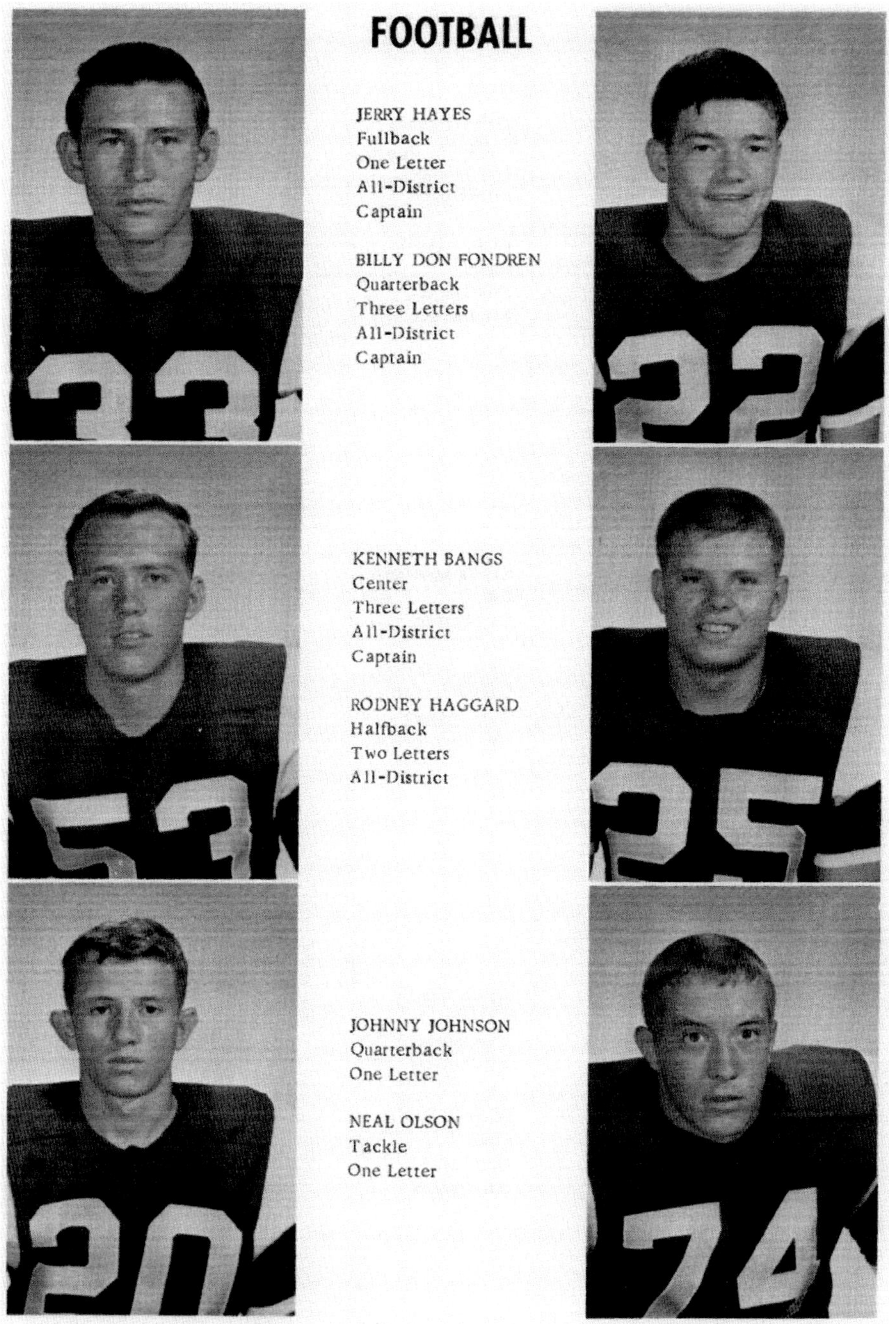

FOOTBALL

JERRY HAYES
Fullback
One Letter
All-District
Captain

BILLY DON FONDREN
Quarterback
Three Letters
All-District
Captain

KENNETH BANGS
Center
Three Letters
All-District
Captain

RODNEY HAGGARD
Halfback
Two Letters
All-District

JOHNNY JOHNSON
Quarterback
One Letter

NEAL OLSON
Tackle
One Letter

Players' football photographs from *The Planonian*.

Chapter 6
VICTORY

The Players

In every sport, you often hear coaches talk about the importance of playing as a team, a unit of talented players working together like a well-oiled machine. But there are always superstar players who rise to the top and shine on the field, in the classroom, in the community and beyond. And their names become a part of city history, state titles and championship records. These names are the stuff of which legends are made.

Ken Bangs

After completing high school, Bangs was recruited to play linebacker at the University of Texas–El Paso, which was then called Texas Western College. Afterward, he eventually became a member of the Dallas Police Department and also worked with the Plano school district.[189] Ken holds a BS in criminal justice from Sam Houston State University, an MS in human relations and management from Amber University and a doctorate of ministry in Christian counseling from Jacksonville Theological Seminary. Ken and his wife, Trudy, are the founders of Gateway Farm, a Christian ministry.

Kenneth Davis

Davis made the Texas all-state squad in 1966 as offensive tackle and the following year played defensive guard when Texas solidly beat the all-state team from Pennsylvania. He was also a standout on Plano's track and field

Players' football photographs from *The Planonian*.

FOOTBALL

STEVE CHRISTIE
End
One Letter

JIMMY MERRIMAN
Halfback
One Letter

MIKE WHEELER
Tackle
One Letter

MIKE JOHNSON
Guard
One Letter

DAVID PETERS
Guard
One Letter

JOHN GRIGGS
Halfback
One Letter

LARRY FAUGHT
Guard
One Letter

Players' football photographs from *The Planonian*.

team, qualifying for the state meet in the one-hundred-yard dash. Davis was an incredible athlete who went on to play multiple positions, including nose guard, offensive tackle and defensive guard, at Coffeyville Junior College and the University of Oklahoma. Unfortunately, he would sustain a career-ending injury in his first year with the Sooners.[190]

Billy Don Fondren

Fondren played quarterback at Texas Christian University from 1967 to 1969. He also punted and played defensive back. In his college years, he would drop "Don" from his name and begin going by Billy Fondren. In 1968, while playing against the University of Texas Longhorns, Fondren completed an eighty-yard interception to give the Horned Frogs their first goal of the game and help shift the momentum.[191]

Johnny Griggs

Plano's all-state running back passed away in 1984 due to a tragic car accident.[192] Former Plano mayor Alton Allman remembers Griggs's impact on the community: "I recall him [Johnny Griggs] quite well. He helped integrate, especially every time he crossed the goal line."[193] Teammate Ken Bangs was close to Johnny Griggs, recalling that he had a propensity to wander a little bit:

> *So when we went to Austin for the state game, Coach Clark called Kenneth Davis and I aside and said, "Y'all are going to sleep three to a bed, and*

Player Johnny Griggs in his yearbook photo.

> *John Griggs is going to sleep between you. And if John Griggs gets out of the bed, I'm coming to you first!" A white teenager sharing a bed with two African American teammates would have been unheard of in 1965... He was* [like] *Duane Thomas* [a former Dallas Cowboy running back]. *But he was young, too...and we would have to talk to him every once in a while. He would get a little down* [and say], *"This is too hard. It's too hard."*[194]

Johnny Robinson

Robinson became a running back for the University of Texas. He was a member on the team when the Longhorns achieved a thirty-game winning streak and went on to become national champions in 1969 and 1970.[195]

A group of players after being awarded All-District honors. *Courtesy of* The Planonian.

Alex Williams

Alex Williams was the first black quarterback to play for the Plano High School Wildcats. Coach Clark described the situation candidly: "They were fine with Johnny running the ball up and down the field and scoring touchdowns, but for some reason, Alex playing quarterback got to them." At least that was the case until the uncertain fans saw what an amazing player Williams was.

Coach Clark implied that the unhappy rumblings about Williams and his black teammates never got too loud, but when he was asked about keeping the black players from quitting, he simply said that the players wouldn't let the other players quit. "We had some guys walk out, and then I said to Johnny and Ken, 'We've never had a kid from the Douglass community quit.' They went out and talked to the other guys, and everybody came back."

After starting at quarterback at Howard Payne University, Williams eventually tried out for the Pittsburgh Steelers but missed the cut.[196] He was an unbelievable overall high school athlete who won district in tennis twice despite never playing in any other matches.

Danny and Gary Minton

When Danny Minton suffered a career-ending neck injury in high school, his younger brother Gary suited up in Danny's uniform for the state championship game. Gary was also a stand-out sprinter for the Wildcats track and field team. The Minton boys' father, Smitty Minton, became stadium manager of Clark Stadium and was always the last to leave and turn off the lights at the stadium until he retired at age eighty-six.[197] Smitty Minton is the Plano Wildcats' "super fan," missing only one Wildcat football game from 1959 to 2009.[198] "He missed his daughter's first child being born because he was in line buying tickets to a Plano football game," said son Terry Minton, who also played football for the Wildcats. "Dad loves being around football, coaches and athletics."[199] The elevator at Clark Stadium has been named "Smitty's Elevator."

Rodney Haggard

Rodney Haggard was an All-District halfback on the 1965 state championship team. After high school, Haggard enrolled at Texas Christian University. An injury to his leg kept him from continuing his football career as a TCU Horned Frog, but he wanted to stay close to the game. "I couldn't play football, so I felt the closest I could get to the field was being a cheerleader," he said.[200]

Early Christmas for End

Plano Gridders Give Game Ball to Injured Minton

By GENE WILSON

It was the happiest Christmas present Danny Minton ever received.

"Thanks fellows," he said Sunday afternoon from his bed at Baylor Hospital when his Plano teammates presented him the state championship game ball. "This is a happy moment for me."

Danny Minton would have liked to have played in the Wildcats' 20-17 victory over Edna Saturday night in Austin.

But he couldn't. He has a broken neck.

Danny's high school football career ended last week when he crashed into an Iowa Park ball carrier. The blow broke his neck and hospitalized him for at least six weeks.

BUT, HIS teammates didn't forget him.

"This is something the boys wanted to do," coach Tom Gray said. "They thought Danny deserved the game ball."

It certainly made him feel proud.

"I'm feeling fine right now," he said. "I'll be here five more weeks. Wasn't it a great game? I thought we played real sound football."

The game wasn't broadcast on local radio, but Danny's mother watched the Wildcat victory, then hurried a call to his room in 6030 and told Danny the news.

"I thought we would win," he said, "but you can't tell when you're playing for the state championship what might happen."

HE ALSO heard a replay from a McKinney radio station earlier Sunday afternoon. "It was a real thrilling game," he added, "I got all involved and found myself kinda playing again."

Danny is a senior, and he hopes to play football in college. "I'm really thinking about it, but I don't know for certain," he said.

It's been a long hard luck season for the 150-pounder. He started the first two games at halfback, but broke his collarbone in the third game and was out of action for four weeks. He shifted to defensive end when he returned.

A twisted ankle kept him out of another game and a hip injury (bad bruise) hobbled him in still another. But, he kept battling back and had become a defensive star until he crashed into that ball carrier from Iowa Park at Wichita Falls last week.

"HE WOULD have played anywhere," said Gray. "Just as long as he could play. That was important to him. He's a fine young man."

There was, however, a Minton suited out Saturday night. Danny's younger brother, Gary, wore Danny's uniform. "We moved him up from the junior varsity so he could suit out for the title game," Gray said.

Plano will graduate 14 men of a 31-man squad, but there is potential for another good team. Halfback Johnny Griggs and defensive star Johnny Robinson head the returnees.

"We're just real thankful for everything," Gray said. "My staff (John Clark, Jack Cockrell, Jake Swann and Sherman Millender) have done a wonderful job. Our support has been tremendous. It's been a year to remember."

Gray hopes to forget everything—at least temporarily. He will take a few days off, go deer hunting before spending the Christmas holidays with his family and friends.

He'll also pay a visit to a fine defensive end in Baylor Hospital.

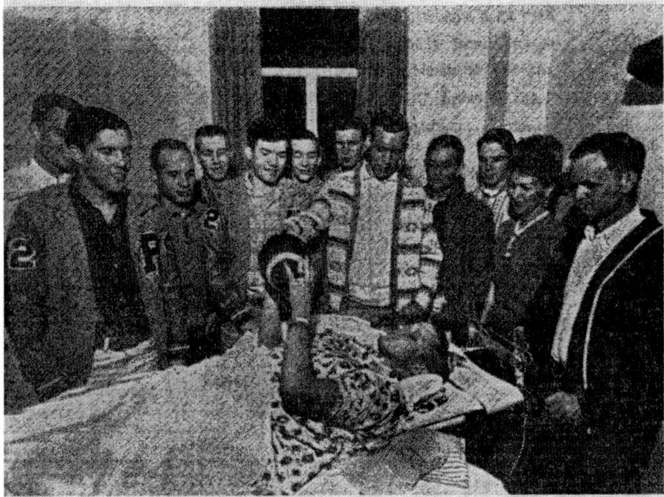

—Dallas News Staff Photo.

Trophy for Fallen Wildcat

Danny Minton, Plano end who suffered a broken neck in semifinals against Iowa Park, Dec. 11, proudly holds ball with which teammates Saturday night won the state Class AA grid championship. The new champs visited their stricken teammate at Baylor Hospital Sunday afternoon and awarded him the game ball. At right are his parents Mr. and Mrs. A. N. (Smitty) Minton. Danny will be hospitalized another month.

A *Dallas Morning News* article and photo featuring the Wildcat team presenting Danny Minton with the game ball after winning state.

Haggard graduated from TCU's M.J. Neeley School of Business in 1970 and went on to become managing partner at Fairview Farm Land Company.

The Haggard family has a long history in Plano, Texas. Clinton Shepard Haggard, born on November 12, 1838, in Winchester, Kentucky, was one of the first pioneer settlers of Plano. At the age of eighteen, he moved to Texas with his father.[201] Visitors traveling around Plano will see the Haggard name all around town—examples include the Haggard Library, Haggard Middle School and Haggard Park, home of Plano's historic Interurban Railway Museum.

These men are only a few of the players who helped to build the powerhouse of today's Plano athletics program. But these individuals deserve special mention specifically due to their influence in regard to integration and the seasons that started the tradition of state champions.

The Games

Football is for everyone. The game wouldn't be the same without the band, the cheerleaders, the dance team, the student players or the fans. Football is, of course, very important for the players and coaches. But it is also a significant and polarizing force for small towns and big cities alike. The games give kids a place to go on Friday nights. Bonds are formed as students of various backgrounds and divergent interests stand side by side to root for their team. Parents have a reason to get to know one another, and alumni have a reason to come back year after year to reminisce and once again cheer on their team.

Plano's Football History Before 1965

Although 1965 was Plano's first state championship, the Wildcats trophy case was not empty. In 1925, Texas high schools did not have the school classifications they do today. The '25 Wildcats played a diverse schedule that included Dallas Terrill Prep, Frisco, Lancaster and their Collin County rivals to the north, McKinney. The Wildcats would go through this schedule undefeated, but unfortunately there was not a state playoff in which they could test their mettle against other Texas teams. The 1925 Wildcats would be the first of many great Wildcat teams.

1903 Harvester Champions, Plano, Texas. *Courtesy of the Interurban Railway Collection.*

The 1934 Wildcats would finish the season with ten wins and just two losses. The only regular-season loss came against rival McKinney. Plano would defeat Fort Worth Trimble Tech in the bi-district playoff before losing to Crowell in the regional playoff.[202]

Two years later, in 1936, the Wildcats would field another powerful team. The season started off on a sour note, though, losing again to rival McKinney, 13–0. The rest of the regular season would see only one other blemish on the schedule, a scoreless tie with Garland. However, the Wildcats once again could not get past the regional round in the playoffs. Plano beat Commerce in the bi-district round (20–0) but then lost to Irving (14–7) in the regional.[203]

In 1939, the Wildcats once again failed to get past the regional round of the state playoffs. Plano suffered only one defeat in the regular season, a 12–0 loss to Garland. The Wildcats also had a tie against Rockwell, a contest in which neither team could score. The Wildcats beat Cooper 31–6 in the bi-district before falling to Mineola in the regional, 29–6.[204]

Overshadowed by Coach Gray's 1965 state championship team are his 1961 and 1963 Wildcats. The 1961 team went through the regular season

A spread of pictures from the state playoff game in *The Planonian*.

undefeated. The Plano defense was solid, allowing opponents an average of fewer than ten points a game. In the bi-district, the Wildcats would defeat Duncanville 28–20. However, they could not overcome the curse of the regional round, succumbing to Jacksboro, 20–12.[205] The 1963 Wildcats had another fantastic season, finishing with nine wins and just one loss and shutting out six of their opponents. Unfortunately, their one loss came against a school in their district, Rockwall. The Yellowjackets would win the district and go on to the playoffs, where they would roll to a state championship. Plano would have to wait two more years to taste the glory of a state championship.[206]

Football is a big, loud game that can also raise awareness of other events taking place on a school's campus. Everybody knows that football is big in Texas, but sometimes it is hard to comprehend just how big it really is. James Thomas, who played football for Plano from 1965 to 1968, has friends who "are still upset that they had bigger, stronger, faster athletes in McKinney than we had in Plano. They knew that we would make a block or two—they expected that they would lose the game. We always expected to win. We were always prepared."[207]

Ronny Hart, a Plano Wildcat from 1962 to 1965, echoed his sentiments: "If Plano is in the ball game at halftime, you're going to get beat. Coaches were going to go in and make adjustments at halftime. You had to beat them in the first half of the game if you were going to win."[208]

However, 1965 brought big opportunities for the Plano High School athletic programs. The school was finally large enough to compete at state levels, and this population increase brought a whole new set of players to the field. Things were about to change. Ken Bangs recalled:

> *When Tom Gray came to Plano, he established a system. He started in the elementary school. When we were in the sixth grade, he started running the Morris D offense and the Morris D defense. At the end of the sixth grade, there was a full-on scrimmage without pads. And Tom Gray was there. He witnessed it. He watched a lot of the workouts during the years with the sixth graders. By the time we were in seventh grade, we knew by heart the audibles, the defense, the sets, the formations. We knew what we were going to run. He drilled it into us over and over and over. When we were in seventh grade, we were undefeated. Our team came together and said, "We will win the state championship when we are seniors." In eighth grade, we lost one game. Freshman year, we were undefeated. I went on to varsity when I was a sophomore. And we were in the playoffs our junior year, but we*

FRESHMAN TEAM — Here's the future Plano High Wildcat varsity team, who are making a good record for themselves this season. Pictured are: FIRST ROW (l. to r.) — Allen Frazier, Mike Loader, Steve Christie, Tommy Skelton, James Smithson, Billy Sangster, Dickie Logan. SECOND ROW — Joe Raines, Mgr.; Jimmy Merriman, Willie Prince, George Jones, Donnie Herrin, David Peters, Larry Faught, Coach Millender. THIRD ROW — Gene Berry, Gary Beard, Johnny Robinson, Wesley Henderson, Joe Steenbergen, and Dean Reed.

This photo of the freshman Wildcat team would be the last before integration on October 23, 1963. *Courtesy of the* Plano Star Courier.

> *lost. Our senior year, that seventh-grade class, we lost one game—it was to Bonham—and won the rest of our games. His method of scouting and preparing for the game...his game plans were so precise that we knew their tendencies and down and distance, and we knew when they came out in their sets and formations.*[209]

1965 Plano Wildcats[210]

Record: 14-1

Plano 27, Decatur 13
Plano 14, Lake Highlands 12
Plano 40, Grapevine 8
Plano 16, Bonham 23 [L]

Plano 34, Lancaster 0
Plano 22, Irving MacArthur 7
Plano 7, Dallas Seagoville 0
Plano 47, Wilmer-Hutchins 0
Plano 34, Lewisville 0
Plano 45, Rockwall 6
Plano 6, West 0
Plano 44, Lake Worth 6
Plano 22, DeKalb 0
Plano 40, Iowa Park 8
Plano 20, Edna 17

Plano Wildcats state championship decal. *Courtesy of the Steve Christie Collection, Haggard Library, Plano, Texas.*

Coach Tom Gray was an enthusiastic advocate of hard work. Whether on the football field, in the halls of the school or out and about in the community, he expected a lot from his players, his coaches and especially from himself. The year 1965 brought racial integration to Plano High School, which meant the football team was integrated as well. Gray took the

—Dallas News Staff Photos by John Flynn..

Plano Gets Ready

These four Plano Wildcats will see action Friday night against the DeKalb Bears at Memorial Stadium in Commerce in a Class AA quarter-finals match. From left to right, it's Kenneth Davis, Rodney Haggard, Kenneth Bangs and Ronnie Davis. (See story, Page 4B.)

The *Dallas Morning News* detailing the Plano team. Included in the photo are (from left to right) Kenneth Davis, Rodney Haggard, Ken Bangs and Ronnie Davis.

transition in stride, managing what could have been a difficult situation with dignity and integrity.

Oral tradition states that Coach Gray sat his team down and said, "There isn't going to be any trouble." And there wasn't. Coach Gray was a tough coach with an old-school style. He expected his players to be the best examples of men both on and off the field. Even if there were tensions, nobody can remember them today because everybody knew they didn't want to anger Coach.[211]

Integration brought new players to the team. There were many new superstars added to the roster that year, as well as many memorable moments. Talented quarterback Billy Don Fondren came strong into the 1965 season after having suffered a broken arm the year before while playing Lancaster.[212] Fondren played both sides of the ball and was also voted most popular boy in school.[213] Another superstar, Kenneth Davis, who was new to the team due to integration, came from a legacy of star athletes. His father was twice voted All-American at Texas Southern. It is said that Davis and his teammates could hear Davis's father yelling to "pick it up" from the sidelines.[214]

The 1965 season was one of many memorable games, amazing plays, astounding injuries and heart-stopping moments. Each game was unforgettable in its own way.

9/3 vs. Decatur (Home)
27–13

Player Johnny Robinson pulled out all the stops during this home game season opener, scoring three touchdowns in a 27–13 win.[215] There were changes on the football field, to be certain, but integration meant changes in the marching band, too, with twenty-eight new members marching in front of an audience for the first time.

9/24 vs. Bonham (Home)
16–23

At this time, Bonham High School's students had a rather boorish tradition that really demonstrated their arrogance on the football field. At the start of each game, their mascot, the Bonham Purple Warrior, would run down the field and end his run by throwing a hatchet through the other team's goal post.[216] Plano took offense to the tradition, and players decided that they weren't going to let such disrespect take place on their home field. One of the Plano High School students grabbed the hatchet from the mascot before it could be thrown through the uprights and took off running. The opposing fans as well as the Bonham team gave chase, but the pursuit ended uneventfully.[217] At this time, pranks like this were considered more or less harmless and simply served as a way to engage the fans of both teams.

10/15 vs. Seagoville (Away)
7–0

In the Wildcats' first away game of the season, dynamo player Johnny Griggs launched himself into the spotlight and became a household name when, on the first play of the game, he carried the ball for a one-hundred-yard touchdown against the Dragons. It turned out to be the only score of the long and muddy game.[218]

100-YARD RUN WINS FOR THE WILDCATS

Star 10-20-65

It was perhaps the longest 100 yards he had ever run in his life — but that important 100-yard dash after the opening kickoff of the Plano - Seagoville game Friday night at Seagoville was undoubtedly the most important 100 yards ever run in recent PLANO High School football history.

Playing on a soggy, muddy field, neither team was able to make any potent scoring plays, and as the game progressed, the 7-0 advantage for Plano grew larger and larger.

But back to that all - important scoring play. Plano received the Seagoville kickoff, and John Grigs, the speedy Plano halfback, was the young man who let the Dragons "have it." He sped the entire length of the field after taking a hand-off from Johnny Pool on the game's opening play. The Wildcat blocking was superb and sprang Griggs loose for his immortal un.

Both Wildcat and Dragon defensive lines played superb ball and frequently bottled up the opposing backfield's thrusts.

Bill Fonden, Plano's speedy quarterback, did complete a beautiful 45-yard pass to End Gene Berry and Fondren was also a factor in Plano's defense with his great punting that often kept the Dragons in the hole.

Among standouts were Kenneth Davis, Jerry Hayes, Kenneth Bangs, Frank Heinen, and many others. They kept the Dragons' famed David King bottled up most of the evening.

The Dragons had opportunities to score, following fumbles deep in Plano territory, but cuuld not take advantage of their opportunities as the Wildcat line dug in to hold the enemy at bay.

For the Dragons, superb defensive work was turned in by Doug Thomas, Jerry Daniels, James Bannister, Tommy Ford and Tommy Hawthorne.

They had much to do in limiting the Wildcats to one lone pass — a 45-yarder and to slihtly less than 100 yards rushing.

Again, the mud had its effect on both teams. On a dry field, the scoring perhaps would have been much higher. And who knows ? Maybe a larger Plano score!

The *Plano Star Courier* headline about Johnny Griggs's one-hundred-yard touchdown in a game against the Dragons.

Opposite: Game program for Seagoville vs. Plano. *Courtesy of the Steve Christie Collection, Haggard Library, Plano, Texas.*

11/19 vs. West (Away)
6–0

The team from West was a major rivalry for the Wildcats. West was a larger team by number of players and by individual player size. However, as was their tradition, the Wildcats fought like crazy. Johnny Griggs ended the game with 108 yards in 24 carries. Kenneth Davis recovered a West fumble

Game program for West Trojans vs. Plano Wildcats. *Courtesy of the Steve Christie Collection, Haggard Library, Plano, Texas.*

on the twelve yard line in the fourth quarter. Fondren intercepted a pass near the end of the game and also completed 9 passes for 231 yards. The Wildcat defense held the West team offense to 88 yards rushing and 104 yards passing.[219]

12/11 vs. Iowa Park (Away)
40–8

Coach Gray called the score of this game "misleading," saying that Iowa Park had played a great game.[220] Before the game started, Iowa Park declared it would "beat the wild out of the Wildcats and send home kittens." There was no doubt that this semifinal game meant a lot to both teams. Some said it was Kenneth Davis's best game of the season. Fatefully, Danny Minton collided with Iowa Park player Dennis Hill and broke his neck. Following the devastating injury, the team visited Minton in the hospital and awarded him the game ball as he lay in a hospital bed. Player Ronny Hart recalled the night of the injury: "That was one of the first really serious injuries that we'd seen." Coach Clark also recalled the visit to the hospital after the game. He was shocked by how large the apparatus was that had been attached to Minton in order to keep his neck straight. As a way to pay honor

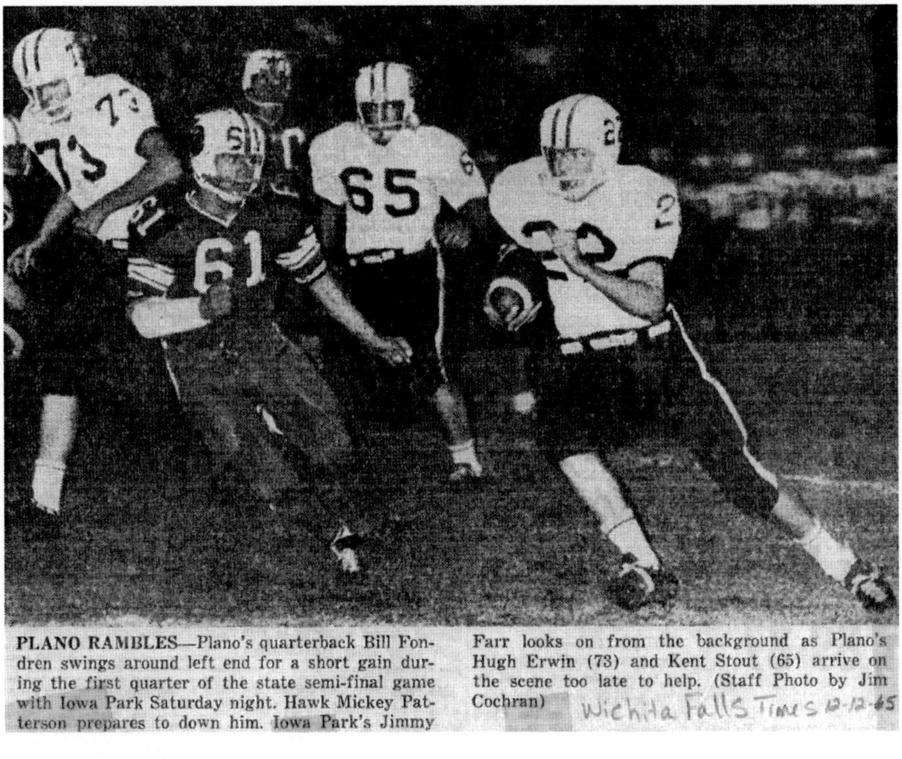

PLANO RAMBLES—Plano's quarterback Bill Fondren swings around left end for a short gain during the first quarter of the state semi-final game with Iowa Park Saturday night. Hawk Mickey Patterson prepares to down him. Iowa Park's Jimmy Farr looks on from the background as Plano's Hugh Erwin (73) and Kent Stout (65) arrive on the scene too late to help. (Staff Photo by Jim Cochran)

Billy Don Fondren carries the ball for a short gain in a game against Iowa Park. *Courtesy of the* Wichita Falls Times.

Plano fans gathering for a pre-game pep rally in the rain in Austin, Texas. *Courtesy of the Steve Christie Collection, Haggard Library, Plano, Texas.*

A sign for fans to hold during the game or parades. *Courtesy of the Steve Christie Collection, Haggard Library, Plano, Texas.*

to Minton missing the last game of the season, Coach Gray had Danny Minton's younger brother Gary suit up in his uniform and join the team on the sidelines for the state championship game against Edna.

12/18 vs. Edna (Championship Game Played at Nelson Field in Austin)
20–17

Coach Gray would later say that this rain-soaked game against Edna was fairly anticlimactic and that his favorite game of the season had been the one

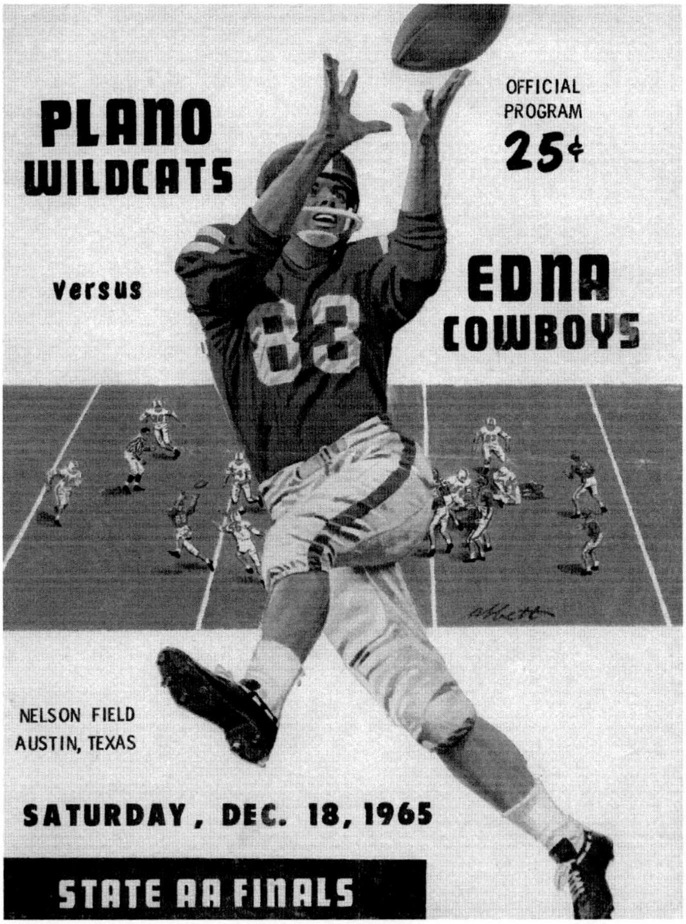

Game program for the AA state finals. *Courtesy of the Steve Christie Collection, Haggard Library, Plano, Texas.*

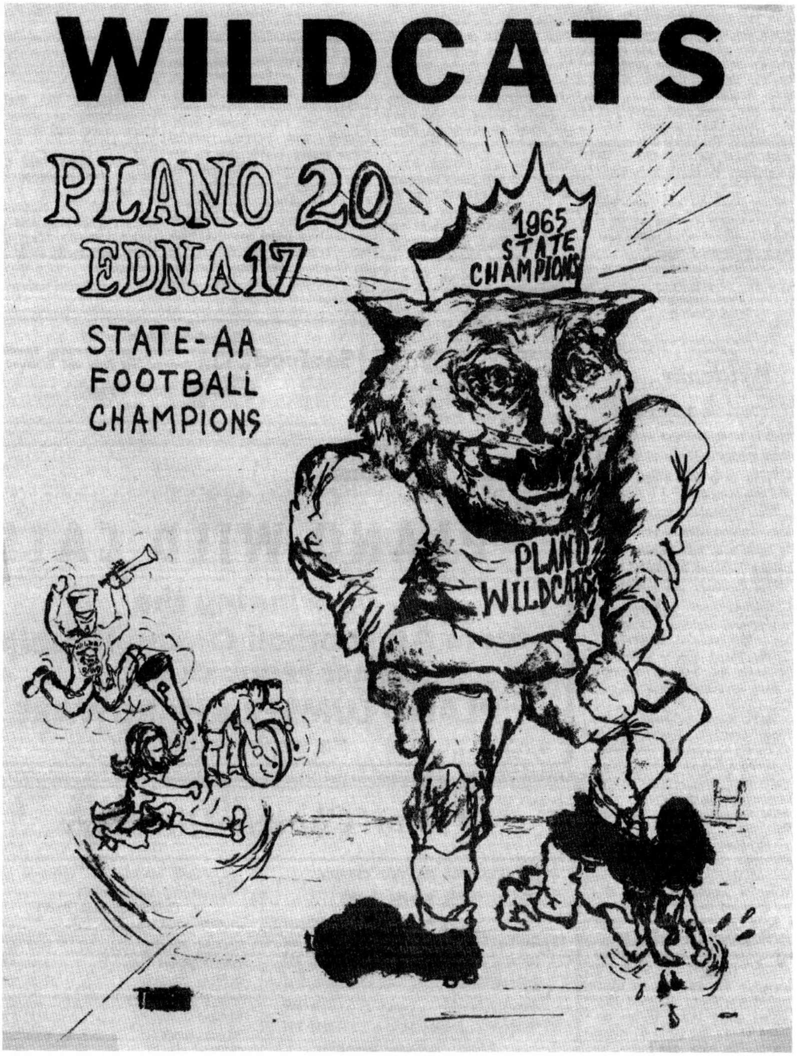

A *Plano Star Courier* editorial cartoon supporting the Plano Wildcats.

against Iowa Park. Throughout the gloomy, gray game, the crowd maintained their raucous support for their Wildcats. It seemed that Coach Gray was the only one who found it less exciting than the previous week's game—the fans were in overdrive! In a strategic move, Coach Gray sent in the word for quarterback Fondren to allow a safety so that the ball could be punted and recovered for a victory. An additional twist to this interesting game was that it was set to be played without a scoreboard, but University of Texas head

PLANO STAR-COU

SOUTH COLLIN'S LARGEST CIRCULATED NEWSPAPER

PLANO, TEXAS, WEDNESDAY, DECEMBER 15, 1965

WILDCATS GO T

Where's Everybody?

Plano 'Ca

Edna In

The rampaging Plano High Wildcat football team advanced to this week's state "AA" finals by virtue of a resounding defeat of highly favored Iowa Park in Wichita Falls Saturday night, 40-6.

Football fever was at an all-time high in Plano early this week and the interest was expected to mount as the week progressed.

On street corners, in local businesses — everywhere fans congregated — there was primarily one and only one subject — Football.

The Wildcats
Edna Cowboys
the Needville
tin — a neutr
day night of tl
p.m.

Site of the g
son Field at
School, which s
The stadiun
north and sou
served seats o
Plano has be
tions A, B and
side, beginning
line and runnir
Edna has o

The front page of the *Plano Star Courier* the Wednesday before the state championship game against Edna.

coach Darrell Royal agreed to let the teams use the basketball scoreboard, which was held up by a forklift at the end of the field.

The 1965 season was successful for Plano High School both on and off the football field. Integration was not without its issues, but the Wildcats seemed to avoid any major hiccups. When John Clark was asked why he thought Plano High School and the surrounding community had such a fruitful evolution into integration, he said he believes the transition was successful because of the mutual effort of community leaders. Coach Clark emphasized the fact that the Douglass community expected a lot from their kids and from the

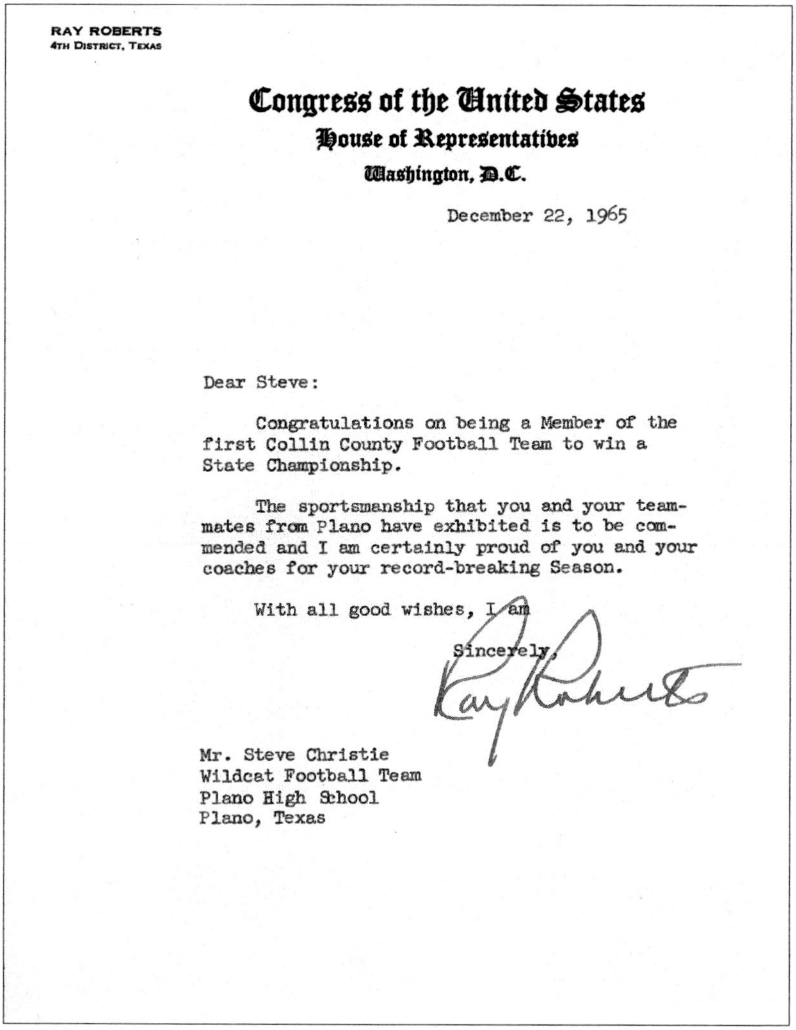

RAY ROBERTS
4TH DISTRICT, TEXAS

Congress of the United States
House of Representatives
Washington, D.C.

December 22, 1965

Dear Steve:

Congratulations on being a Member of the first Collin County Football Team to win a State Championship.

The sportsmanship that you and your teammates from Plano have exhibited is to be commended and I am certainly proud of you and your coaches for your record-breaking Season.

With all good wishes, I am

Sincerely,

Ray Roberts

Mr. Steve Christie
Wildcat Football Team
Plano High School
Plano, Texas

Congressman Ray Roberts wrote a congratulatory letter to Steve Christie after the Wildcats' 1965 state championship. *Courtesy of the Steve Christie Collection, Haggard Library, Plano, Texas.*

larger opportunities that were becoming available to everyone. Douglass community leaders worked with the school and athletic department leaders in order to ensure understanding and mutual success. Did Coach Clark and Coach Gray realize their place in leading the race relations in the city and in the school? Coach Clark said, in classic coach style, "I wasn't trying to be a leader in race relations; I just wanted the best players out there."[221]

DAY, DECEMBER 22, 1965 NO. 16

WIN STATE

Plano Is First Collin Team To Win State Title

By JERRY SMITH

Christmas was still a week away, but Santa Claus made an early trip to Austin, Dec. 18 and gave the Plano Wildcats their first State AA Championship, gift - wrapped in a 20-17 victory over the Edna Cowboys.

Although the outcome of the game was in doubt until versatile Bill Fondren plucked a Cowboy aerial late in the game, all the faithful knew the Wildcats would win because Santa Claus had already demonstrated in favor of Plano.

The Wildcats found that the ball was almost harder to handle in the first half than were the Cowboys. The PHS team fumbled its first two possessions, enabling Edna to jump off to an early 8-0 lead.

Following Jimmy Curlee's fumble recovery on the PHS 29 yard line, the previously undefeated Cowboys needed but four plays to score. Halfback Danny McBride tallied from four yards out and then added the extra points.

The Wildcats came roaring right back into the teeth of the north wind for their first score. Rodney Haggard's 40 yard kickoff return and a roughing penalty set up the Wildcats on the Cowboy 41 yard line.

Plano's hard - running trio of John Griggs, Jerry Hayes and Bill Fondren pounded out the yardage. Fondren, faking beautifully, pranced 12 yards into the end zone for the score with 1:45 left in the first quarter.

The second Plano score early in the second quarter was set up by a short Cowboy punt to the PHS 44 yard line.

Griggs picked up 12 yards and a roughing penalty moved the ball to the 17 yard marker. Fondren picked his way into the end zone on the next play for the score. Griggs' extra points gave PHS a 14-8 lead with 8:18 left till half.

The Wildcats again made tracks for the Cowboy goal following another short punt. Jerry Hayes dove over from the one to close out Plano's scoring. . . .Fondren's 13 yard dash to the one was the big gainer on the drive.

The second half was an entirely different ball game. The potent Edna offense, which had been bottled up the first half, moved into the high gear while the Cowboy defense clamped down on the Wildcats.

The Cowboys began their longest drive of the night at their own 20 late in the third quarter. The Wildcats grudgingly gave up short yardage for the remainder of the quarter.

On the first play of the fourth quarter, relief quarterback Tommy Miller rolled to his right and hurried 44 yards down the side line for the score. Dennis Whitley's extra point kick cut the Plano lead to 20-15.

The Wildcats still were not

Continued on Page 2

Plano Star Courier article referencing the Wildcat victory.

1966 Plano Wildcats[222]

Record: 11-1

Plano 30, Ennis 6
Plano 28, Bonham 7
Plano 23, Lancaster 6
Plano 40, Terrell 6
Plano 6, Decatur 7 [L]
Plano 59, Wilmer-Hutchins 0 (District)
Plano 51, Rockwall 0 (District)
Plano 41, Desoto 6 (District)
Plano 34, Dallas Seagoville 0 (District)

Plano 41, Mexia 7 (District)
Plano 14, Decatur 6 (Regional)
Plano 15, Dangerfield 21 (Quarterfinal)

11/19 vs. Mexia (Away)
41–7

This bi-district game was said to be Johnny Robinson's best of the season, as he collected 240 yards in the contest. Mexia entered the matchup with a record of 10-0. The score was 41–0 at the end of the first half, and starters didn't play in the second half.

Yearbook photo of the regional champs. *Courtesy of* The Planonian.

12/02 vs. Dangerfield (Away)
15–21

This was a stunning, heartbreaking loss for Plano. When the seemingly undefeatable Wildcats were beaten by Dangerfield, it resonated. The Wildcat team would seek vengeance against this opponent in the following year. Despite the end result of a loss, the team did fight hard in this game, and Griggs managed a ninety-three-yard touchdown run.

1967 Plano Wildcats

Plano 2, Ennis 14 [L]
Plano 28, Bonham 0

Plano 16, Greenville 13
Plano 37, Lancaster 12
Plano 35, Decatur 7
Plano 34, Richardson Hamilton Park 26 (District)
Plano 41, Hutchins Kennedy 0 (District)
Plano 29, Rockwall 0 (District)
Plano 33, Forney 6 (District)
Plano 26, Desoto 0 (District)
Plano 35, Mexia 7 (Bi-district)
Plano 28, Decatur 0 (Regional)
Plano 14, Daingerfield 7 (Quarterfinal)
Plano 15, Philips 13 (Semifinal)
Plano 27, University City Randolph 8 (Final)

10/27 vs. Rockwall (Away)
29–0

Rockwall and Plano had a long-standing rivalry. The Rockwall Yellowjackets beat Plano in the 1963 regular season on the way to their first state championship. With division changes, this game was the last in a thirty-eight-game series dating back to 1919. The fierce rivalry ignited Plano's

Community parade with Plano cheerleaders. *Courtesy of* The Planonian.

passion for their Wildcats. It seemed that everyone in the small community had some sort of attachment to the matchup. Parades and celebrations were planned around the game even though it wasn't a truly "big" game on the schedule. At this matchup, the Plano band played the song "Joshua Fought the Battle of Jericho," and Plano fans yelled, "…and the (Rock) Walls come tumbling down!"

11/10 vs. Desoto (Away)
28–0

This was a big matchup due to the fact that Plano's team had earned the title of northern division champs and Desoto had been crowned the southern division champs. Despite the fact that the field was incredibly soggy, Johnny Griggs ran for three touchdowns, and quarterback Alex Williams had a twenty-one-yard touchdown run. It was a decisive victory for the Wildcats, and one of the Desoto players ended up getting knocked out by a strong double block by Plano players.

12/1 vs. Dangerfield (Away)
14–7

After the heartbreak of the year before, the Wildcats were determined to emerge victorious after this game. This game was played at Lobo Field in Longview in front of a crowd of eleven thousand people. Again, two rivals met, but this time the outcome was much different as the Wildcats advanced in their quest for state championship.

12/15 vs. San Antonio Randolph (Away at Baylor Stadium in Waco)
27–8

Now a well-known Plano athlete, Johnny Griggs made an immediate impact in this game, scoring an early sixty-six-yard touchdown seconds after the start of the game. Williams and Griggs upped their superstar status in this game, both scoring two touchdowns with long runs. On the second play of the second half, Alex Williams completed a forty-five-yard run. On the next play, he completed a pass to Freddie McEntyre to retake the lead. Williams added a ninty-four-yard dash for the third touchdown, and Griggs scored the final touchdown, solidifying the 27–8 victory.

The 1967 state champion Wildcats. *Courtesy of* The Planonian.

In a 2009 radio interview, Coach Clark stated that he remembered the field being wet and everybody sliding all over the place during this game—everybody, that is, except his backs, who always played great in the mud! Coach Clark also joked that there was an army base out there, and he wasn't sure how it happened, but if the guys' sons were good at football they always ended up transferred to San Antonio.

1971 Plano Wildcats[223]

Plano 26, Richardson Pearce 0
Plano 14, Greenville 16
Plano 24, Lancaster 7
Plano 49, Lewisville 0 (District)
Plano 69, North Garland 0 (District)
Plano 41, Bonham 0 (District)
Plano 53, South Grand Prairie 6 (District)
Plano 7, McKinney 0 (District)
Plano 41, Richardson Berkner 8 (District)
Plano 41, Gainesville 0 (District)
Plano 40, Azle 7 (Bi-district)

Plano 18, Jacksonville 17 (Quarterfinal)
Plano 10, Brownwood 8 (Semifinal)
Plano 21, Gregory Portland 20 (Final)

By this season, the story of integration no longer felt new or awkward. It had become part of the fabric of the community. Player Ronny Hart said, "It just felt like a fit" and that the parents saw it working "and let it work." Player James Thomas said that as a kid, it really felt like a "seamless transition." There were quality teachers, and there was good leadership. "When we arrived, we wondered if there really would be opportunity, and there was for everyone," said Thomas. "Both communities were able to come together because they had been taught separately that if you respect others, they will respect you in return. The coaches made sure the teammates acted right. School integration wasn't the start of integration in Plano. There was already association through work. The kids and the communities could see that bringing the schools together would be a positive thing. At the time, we didn't think we were being progressive; we were just benefiting from leaders with integrity, and that leadership extended out through aspects of the whole community."[224]

Hart echoed Thomas's sentiments, saying that race didn't matter to playing or coaching because "football is about the team; there are no individuals on the field."

Jack and Norma Williams lived in the Douglass community, and their son Jackie was a member of the 1971 state title team. Jackie would go on to play football at Texas A&M and in the NFL for the Buffalo Bills. "Coach Clark—he was the best thing to happen to Plano at the time," said Jackie. "After integration in 1964, they won the first state championship with Coach Clark as an assistant."[225] "He definitely helped. All the kids liked him, black and white," Norma said. "He related with those boys so well, and if he felt they were right, he would defend them."[226]

Coach Clark said that football is a unique window into the dynamics of a high school and that a high school is a unique window into the dynamics of a town. Perhaps this is why Texas communities often look to the leadership of their local coaches. They know their kids, and they know what their kids need.

12/11 vs. Brownwood (Away)
10–8

Clark later said that this game was his most memorable coaching moment. In this game, Plano came from behind to defeat the Brownwood team, which had knocked them out of the playoffs the year before. Determined to seek revenge, the Wildcats fought for victory, and the two teams exchanged touchdowns all the way up until the final moments of the game. Plano scored first on a fifteen-yard pass from Jeff Brumbaugh to tight end Van Davis. A Brownwood tailback then scored, and the Lions successfully completed a two-point conversion. The Wildcats moved the ball down the field with two completed passes, giving Pat Thomas an opportunity to kick the game-winning field goal with twenty-one seconds left in the game. Thomas put it through the uprights, and the Wildcats gave Brownwood its first-ever loss in a regional game.

12/18 vs. Gregory-Portland (Away in Austin)
21–20

Played at Austin Memorial Stadium in Austin, Texas, this championship game was a story of extra points. After Gregory-Portland missed an extra point, Pat Thomas connected for his fourth extra point of the game. Gregory-Portland then attempted a field goal with only fourteen seconds left in the game. The kick missed, and the Wildcats claimed a 21–20 victory. One of the Gregory-Portland players, Marty Akins, who played his final year in 1971, was inducted into the Texas High School Sports Hall of Fame in 1992. Coach Ray Akins, who was in control of the Gregory-Portland team from 1950 to 1988, would also be inducted into the Texas High School Sports Hall of Fame in 1992. Akins was a successful coach, and this added to the Wildcats' excitement of defeating his team for the state championship. Coach Clark said that his guys kept pressure on the kicker throughout the entire game, and that pressure is probably what led to the Wildcats' victory.

1987 Season—High School Football National Champions

Following a legacy of division and state championships, the National Sports News Service Poll awarded the Plano Wildcat program with the title of High School Football National Champions in 1987 based on their record and strength of schedule. At that time, Plano had more D1 scholarships than any other high school football program in the nation.

By this time, football was no longer the only success story in Plano athletics. The girls' soccer and swim teams were also state champions. Coach Clark left a lasting impression in the city and beyond, imparting a legacy of determination and excellence. He impressed on everyone the idea that Plano athletic programs strive for a check in the win column, but only when it is a win for the kids.

Many have said that Coach Clark "brought out the best in you" and that players and others "did what he expected you to do." Plano's current athletic superintendent, Gerald Brence, who is a contemporary educator with some distance from segregation, was asked why football seemed to be one of the first areas to integrate. Brence said that when you coach, you are with your kids every day. "You are looking for good kids and good players," he said. "You don't have time to notice skin color. Time is spent getting to know kids and their families. Football is one of those things that really can bring a community together."[227] Brence also said that Coach Clark's policies inspired the foundations of today's Plano athletics program and that the entire program and school system focuses on the same policy: "Take pride in respect."[228]

Chapter 7

LIVING THE DREAM

The Plano Wildcats of 1965–67 would lay the foundation for one of the greatest dynasties in the history of Texas high school football. As of 2014, only the Celina Bobcats (eight state championships) and the Southlake Carroll Dragons (also with eight state championships) can surpass the Wildcats' seven Texas state titles.

What makes a football dynasty? A football dynasty always has great players, great coaches and fan support, but one of the key elements is stability. The Plano Wildcats share the concept of stability with their big brothers in the NFL, the Pittsburgh Steelers. From 1969 to 2014, the Pittsburgh Steelers have had only three head coaches and have won six Super Bowls with numerous playoff appearances. Likewise, from 1959 to 2014, the Plano Wildcats have had only five head coaches and have won seven Texas state championships and one national championship to go along with numerous playoff appearances. Since Coach Gray was hired in 1959, every succeeding head coach has been selected from the Plano football coaching staff.

The Wildcats secured their third state championship in 1971 with a 21–20 win over Gregory-Portland High School at Memorial Stadium in Austin, Texas. This would be Coach Clark's second and last state championship. The 1971 team also produced one of Plano's greatest players, Pat Thomas. Pat was an All-American at Texas A&M,[229] where he helped Coach Emory Bellard's Aggies to a 10-2 record in 1975. In 1976, Pat was drafted by the Los Angeles Rams, where he would be named All-Pro in 1978 and 1980.

Wildcat players named to the All-District team. *From left to right*: Gene Berry, Tommy Skelton, Alan Frazier, Randall Chaddick, Freddie McIntyre, Johnny Griggs, Kenneth Davis, Mike Wheeler, Johnnie Robinson, Albert Hilburn and Donnie Herrin. *Courtesy of* The Planonian.

Ken Bangs remembers a youthful Pat Thomas: "There was a tradition after a ball game…Pat Thomas would run out and say, 'Can I have your chin strap?' And he had so many of my chin straps that Coach Gray said, "Give away another one, and you're paying them back!'" Bands added, "I played cornerback at division one. You are beat at the snap at that level if you run a 4.5 [a forty-yard dash timed in seconds]. But Pat Thomas was not. I could outrun Pat Thomas—I know I could outrun him. But he had it. He was a quarterback in high school. He kicked a winning field goal against Brownwood in the state championship. He just…Coach Clark told me that Pat came to the sideline when he called time-out and said, 'Coach, don't make me kick it.' And he said, 'Go kick it, Pat.'"[230]

John Lewis, whose wife taught Pat Thomas in high school, recalled:

> *My wife was a teacher at Plano in 1968–69, and Pat Thomas was a freshman or sophomore. My wife comes in—and she is just a real straight arrow—and says, "He's really arrogant—he runs around and he acts like he owns the building. He just acts like he owns the building!" I said, "You know that he really does?" His family goes back to my earliest history of*

> *Plano. I don't know if Ben, his uncle and his grandfather were grooming him for leadership. I don't know if Dr. Hendrick was using Patrick as a cohesive member of society on the school campus, but people really loved and respected Pat Thomas. As Pat Thomas goes, so goes the community. This was a young man that was sixteen or seventeen years old and already enjoyed that kind of reputation and already had that respect from both sides of the community.*[231]

Pat Thomas was an All-Pro in the NFL at the height of five feet, nine inches. John Lewis once asked Pat how he had such success in the NFL: "We were working out one day…and we were talking, and I said, 'Pat, how do you play against six-foot-five players?' He said, 'Lines, angles and planes and leverage!' He gave me a business class on the football field."[232]

One of Plano's biggest rivals for state honors was Brownwood High School and Coach Gordon Wood. Wood is a Texas high school football legend, having won nine state championships and 396 victories overall. Forney coach Kevin Rush remembers Coach Wood telling him about some gamesmanship by John Clark, his counterpart at Plano, before they met in a playoff game in the early 1970s. "Coach Clark had cut out all the plays that [Plano's star player] Pat Thomas had played at quarterback," Rush said. "He didn't even know Pat Thomas played quarterback. Plano beat them. Gordon always said that was one of the state championships he should have won."

Of course, Clark, who still attends Plano games, has his own version of events. "I don't know many coaches who felt like they got an advantage over him [Gordon] in the filming business—and I've talked to a lot of them," Clark said. "Somehow, Gordon's films would be at a college or somewhere, you know. He couldn't get his hands on the films that you felt like would help your team the most. There are stories on both sides."[233]

In 1977, John Clark Field (now known as John Clark Stadium) opened. It was named after the man who brought two state championships to Plano. It was only fitting that the Plano Wildcats' first season at John Clark Field would result in the school's fourth state championship. The Wildcats defeated Port Neches Grove 13–10 at Texas Stadium in Irving, home of the Dallas Cowboys.

The year 1977 is also known for the "Miracle Game" against the Highland Park Scots. The game took place on December 3 at Texas Stadium before a crowd of close to forty thousand fans. After falling into a 28–0 hole, the Wildcats dug their way out and snatched a 29–28 victory.

At halftime, Plano trailed 21–0, and unfortunately things only got worse as the Scots scored a quick touchdown to start the second half. The Wildcat

Plano's first state championship team was the 1965 Wildcats.

Plano's football rich in tradition

Wildcats holders of four state titles

On September 1, 1983, the *Plano Star Courier* ran an article about the first team to hold the title of state champion. By this time, the Wildcats had four state titles.

offense rallied for two scores in the second half, but victory still seemed out of reach. Then the miracle started when Plano defender Carl Smith intercepted a Highland Park pitchout and raced sixty-six yards to cut the deficit to seven. The Scots were determined to run out the clock but had to give the ball back to Plano. With just thirty-three left in the game, prospects looked grim for the Wildcats. However, Perry Haynes caught a flea flicker from Stevie Haynes, and sixty-one yards later, Plano had another touchdown, cutting the deficit to one. Plano lined up for the two-point conversion, and Steve Ulmer went into the end zone standing. The final score was Plano 29, Highland Park 28!

It was also a banner year for Plano's home county, as Collin County nearly had three state champions in '77. The Wiley Pirates defeated Bellville 22–14 to claim the 2A state title to go along with Plano's 4A championship. "When the bus rolled into Pirate Stadium just before ten o'clock on December 17, a throng of ecstatic Wylie fans waited there to greet them. In the crowd were many Plano football fans, who earlier that day had watched their team wrap up the Class 4A state championship, 13–10, over Port Neches Grove at Texas Stadium in Irving. One of the local newspapers reported that the Plano fans at Texas Stadium erupted into cheers for their Collin County neighbors when the final score of the Wylie-Bellville game was announced."[234] Farmersville (northeast of Plano) had a chance to be Collin County's third state champion. The Fightin' Farmers won their district but lost 14–6 in the regional championship against Pottsboro.

Billy Ray Smith Jr., former Plano Wildcat, playing for the University of Arkansas. *Courtesy of University of Arkansas.*

There was hope of a repeat in 1978. The team was led by the son of NFL All-Pro and Super Bowl champion Billy Ray Smith. Smith Jr. would go on to make a name for himself, first as an All-American for the University of Arkansas Razorbacks and then as an All-Pro for the NFL's San Diego Chargers. Sadly, the 1978 Plano Wildcats would have to settle for runner-up status, as they lost the state title to Houston Stratford, 29–13. It was practically a home game for Houston Stratford, as it was played at the "Eighth Wonder of the World," the Houston Astrodome.

It would be eight years before the Plano Wildcats made another appearance in the state championship game, and the Wildcats made the best of their opportunity. The fifth championship would be claimed in 1986 at the Home of the Texas Aggies, Kyle Field in College Station. Plano defeated La Marque 24–7.

Due to the rapid growth of Plano, another high school, Plano East Senior High School, was opened in 1980. The Plano East Panthers would not compete in varsity football until 1982.

Head coach and former Plano Wildcat assistant Jack Swann led the Panthers into competition. The first "Cat Fight" was on November 11, 1982, with the Wildcats defeating Plano East 14–13.

Plano coach Tom Kimbrough was not in favor of Plano Independent School District splitting into two high schools. "I said that if they want to open a second school, I'd be for it if all the boys went to Plano and all the girls to Plano East," said Kimbrough, who was in his fortieth year in the Plano Independent School District athletic department.[235]

In 1987, the Wildcats would earn their second consectutive state championship and claim their sixth state title overall. The title game would be a rematch of the 1978 battle with Houston Stratford. This time, however, the game was held at Memorial Stadium in Austin, and Plano would come out on top, 28–21. The National Sports News Service proclaimed the Wildcats the 1987 High School Football National Champions.

Coach Kimbrough's final season would be 1991. When Wildcat assistant coach Gerald Brence took the reins of the Wildcat football program in 1992, he had big shoes to fill. Thc thrcc prcvious Wildcat coaches had all won at least one state championship. It would not be long before Brence had the Plano Wildcats competing for state championships again. In 1993, the Wildcats were state runner-up, losing 36–13 to Converse Judson at Floyd Casey Stadium in Waco.

In 1994, Plano captured the elusive seventh state championship. In the state semifinals, the Wildcats defeated Texas powerhouse Odessa Permian's Mojo 10–0. Then, in the state championship, played at Texas A&M's Kyle Field, Plano bested another Texas giant, Katy, 28–7.

In 1999, Plano West High School opened due to the continued increase in the area's population. This would serve as a severe blow to the Wildcat program, as it lost many players to the new school. Due to the split, Plano suffered through its first winless season in 2003. The young men who endured through that season of many losses became seniors in 2005. The Wildcats piled up the victories that year, culminating with an undefeated regular season. Entering the playoffs with confidence and momentum, the Wildcats won three playoff games before losing to eventual state champion Southlake Carroll.

Coach Brence would wrap up his coaching career in 2007 with a record of 120-70-2 and was named the Texas Coach of the Year in 1993 and 2005. After relinquishing his head coaching duties, Brence accepted the position of athletic director for the Plano Independent School District.

When asked about his greatest accomplishment as Plano's head coach, Coach Brence did not mention the state championship, instead saying, "The relationships trump the winning and the losing. I feel fortunate that I have so many friends—people I care about and who I know care about me and my family. Every day that I get older, I understand that more. Sometimes I think we need to talk about that a little bit more. Plano is a great place. It will always be my home, but this is a fast-paced town with high achievers, and sometimes it's good that we slow down and talk about the important things."[236]

In 2008, Jaydon McCullough took over the reins of the Plano football program. Coach McCullough has a long history with the Plano program. McCullough played football for the Wildcats in 1979 and 1980 under then head coach Tom Kimbrough. For sixteen years, he was an assistant for the Wildcats before accepting the head coaching position. "It's just an awesome responsibility," McCullough said. "A lot of pressure comes with it. There are high expectations here. I see it as an opportunity. That's the way I have to approach it."[237]

In Coach McCullough's first six seasons, he led the Wildcats to five Texas UIL 5A state playoff appearances. Two of those seasons Plano

Coach Gray and some of his starters pose for a local paper. *Courtesy of the Steve Christie Collection, Haggard Library, Plano, Texas.*

A photograph from a 1965 *Plano Star Courier* article showcasing the star football players and head cheerleaders.

reached the area finals, and three years the team advanced to the Bi-District Championship.

Plano Independent School District athletic director Gerald Brence reflected on the cornerstone laid by Plano's first integrated teams: "We use the same policies that Clark and Gray used in the '60s. There is no place for profanity—look the coach in the eye [and say] 'yes sir' and 'no sir.' Those are really basic things that we are really proud of. We bring in forty-five to fifty new coaches every year, men and women."

Brence also discussed race and sports: "I think that when you get in there with the kids on a daily basis, you really don't see color. You really don't think about it. You look for the best players, and they have to be good kids. Character counts. It falls into place. You just don't see color. It really isn't much of a factor."[238]

The idea of a racially mixed football team was slow to be accepted in the Plano community. But Coach Clark talked about the football team as a catalyst for change in the community:

The All-District team. *From back left to front right*: Ronnie Davis, Johnny Pool, Kent Stout, Ken Bangs, Jerry Hayes, Hugh Erwin, Johnny Robinson, Kenneth Davis, Carl Grey, Billy Don Fondren and Rodney Haggard. *Courtesy of* The Planonian.

> *The acceptance went out to the community from the school. The young people that came together for the program and for the school did very well. It took a while for our fans to say, "This is our team." It took a while to convince them that we could play and win with a black quarterback. There was some opposition...but it was not a problem for coaches. Football is such a picture window of Plano schools. Cheerleaders, the band, the community—everyone is involved. People can see through that what is happening at the schools.*[239]

Coach Clark remembers the night he felt the whole community got behind the idea of an integrated football team:

> *There was a group having a hard time accepting a black quarterback in the community. It was okay with Griggs running in the backfield. We were playing, and Alex* [Alex Williams, Plano's first African American quarterback] *runs for a thirty- to forty-yard score, and when he does, he pulls his hip and limps off the field. We kept him off the field until half-time. We came back out, and he stayed in the dressing room with Dr. Apple. We came back on the field and didn't move the ball very well. Dr. Apple*

The John Clark Stadium and athletic offices in Plano, Texas, were named in honor of Coach John Clark. *Courtesy of Kirby Stokes.*

> *came back on the field with Alex at nearly the end of the third quarter. We put him back in, and the whole stadium went crazy with clapping.*[240]

As former player James Thomas stated, "Friday nights are important [to the Plano community]."[241] Thomas was one of Plano's first African American players, and he talked fondly about the "Plano way":

> *One thing that all of our coaches bring to the table is impeccable integrity. I have been really impressed with the kind of people, the kind of leadership that we have in this community. They know who the kids are; they know who the parents are. It makes a difference. As an African American, I feel blessed to have grown up in Plano. It wasn't like that everywhere. A lot of people that I saw in college brought a lot of baggage with them. We feel blessed that we grew up in a progressive city. At the time, we didn't feel like it was progressive—it just was how it was.*[242]

NOTES

Chapter 1

1. Examiner.com, "Early History of Plano."
2. Ibid.
3. Ibid.
4. The Plano Conservancy for Historic Preservation, Inc., "Discovering Old Plano."
5. Wikipedia, "Plano, Texas."
6. Ibid.
7. Texas State Historical Association, "PLANO, TX."
8. The Plano Conservancy for Historic Preservation, Inc., "Discovering Old Plano."
9. Ibid.
10. Ibid.
11. Ibid.
12. Ibid.
13. Ibid.
14. Texas State Historical Association, "PLANO, TX."
15. The Plano Conservancy for Historic Preservation, Inc., "Discovering Old Plano."
16. Friends of the Plano Public Library, *Plano, Texas*, 191.
17. Interview by author, April 29, 2014.
18. Ibid.
19. Ibid.
20. Ibid.

21. Ibid.
22. Ibid.
23. Ibid.
24. Interview by author, February 19, 2014.
25. Ibid.
26. Interview by author, April 29, 2014.
27. Ibid.
28. Hixson, "King's Local Legacy."
29. Ibid.
30. Interview by author, April 29, 2014.
31. Ibid.
32. Ibid.
33. Ibid.
34. Ibid.
35. Ibid.
36. Ibid.

Chapter 2

37. Ibid.
38. YouTube, "Annie Heads Rainwater."
39. Ibid.
40. Ibid.
41. *Dallas Morning News*, "R.L. Turner Alumni Look Back."
42. Ibid.
43. Ibid.
44. Ibid.
45. Leszcynski, "Garland ISD's Changing Demographics."
46. Ibid.
47. Ibid.
48. *Dallas Morning News*, "R.L. Turner Alumni Look Back."
49. Ibid.
50. Ibid.
51. Ibid.
52. Ibid.
53. Ibid.
54. Ibid., "Lifelong McKinney Residents Recall Overcoming Segregation."
55. Ibid.
56. BlackPast.org, "Fort Worth, Texas."
57. Ibid.
58. Ibid.

59. Ibid.
60. Ibid.
61. Ibid.
62. Ibid.
63. Ibid.
64. Ibid.
65. Ibid.
66. Texas State Historical Association, "MANSFIELD SCHOOL DESEGREGATION INCIDENT."
67. Ibid.
68. Ibid.
69. Ibid.
70. *Dallas Morning News*, "Quiet Man Set off Long, Loud Battle."
71. Advocate Mag, "40 Years of DISD Desegregation."
72. Ibid.
73. Ibid.
74. Ibid.
75. Ibid.
76. Ibid.
77. University of Texas, "Campus Profile."
78. Ibid.
79. Scarborough, "From Black and White to Color."
80. Ibid.
81. Ibid.
82. Ibid.
83. Ibid.
84. Ibid.
85. Thurman, "History of Integration."
86. Biel, "Integration of Stephen F. Austin University."
87. Ibid.
88. Ibid.
89. Ibid.
90. Ibid.
91. Ibid.
92. Ibid.
93. Ibid.
94. Ibid.
95. Ibid.
96. Wikipedia, "Lubbock, Texas."
97. Ibid.
98. Ibid.
99. Scott, "Hardaway Relates Tech Experience."

100. Ibid.
101. Ibid.
102. Ibid.
103. Ibid.
104. Wikipedia, "Houston."
105. University of Houston, "UH at a Glance."
106. Ibid.
107. Wikipedia, "Historical Events of Houston."
108. University of Houston, "UH at a Glance."
109. Jones, "Black History Month."
110. Ibid.
111. Powers, "Silent Transformation in the Bayou City."

Chapter 3

112. Wikipedia, "Brown v. Board of Education."
113. Ibid., "Plano Senior High School."
114. Ibid.
115. Interview by author, April 29, 2014.
116. Ibid.
117. Ibid.
118. Ibid.
119. Ibid.
120. Ibid.
121. Ibid.
122. Ibid.
123. Ibid.
124. Ibid.
125. Ibid.
126. Ibid.
127. Ibid.
128. Ibid.
129. Ibid.
130. Friends of the Plano Public Library, *Plano, Texas*, 183.
131. Interview by author, April 29, 2014.
132. Ibid.
133. Ibid.
134. Ibid.
135. Ibid.
136. Ibid.
137. Ibid.

138. Ibid.
139. Ibid.
140. Ibid.
141. Interview by author, February 19, 2014.
142. Ibid.
143. Interview by author, May 31, 2014.
144. Ibid.
145. Ibid.
146. Ibid.

Chapter 4

147. Hageland, "Losing a Legend."
148. Ibid.
149. Benne, *Best High School Football in the Country*, 20.
150. Interview by author, February 19, 2014.
151. Hasson, "Mesquite Football History."
152. Smith, "Playing in the Cotton Bowl."
153. Hageland, "Losing a Legend."
154. Ibid.
155. Ibid.
156. Interview by author, April 29, 2014.
157. Ibid.
158. Hageland, "Losing a Legend."
159. Benne, *Best High School Football in the Country*, 21.
160. Interview by author, February 19, 2014.
161. Ibid.
162. Ibid.
163. Benne, *Best High School Football in the Country*, 21.
164. Plano Independent School District, "Kimbrough Ranked Among 'Top 10.'"
165. Truesdell, "*Friday Night Lights* Star Returns to PISD."
166. Interview by author, February 19, 2014.
167. Interview by author, April 29, 2014.
168. Ibid.
169. Plano Independent School District, "Kimbrough Ranked Among 'Top 10.'"
170. Ibid.
171. Benne, *Best High School Football in the Country*, 22.
172. Plano Independent School District, "Kimbrough Ranked Among 'Top 10.'"

173. Campbell, "Tradition a Winner at Plano."
174. Benne, *Best High School Football in the Country*, 22.

Chapter 5

175. Wikipedia, "Plano Senior High School."
176. Ibid.
177. Benne, *Best High School Football in the Country*, 28.
178. Ibid.
179. Interview by author, April 29, 2014.
180. Benne, *Best High School Football in the Country*, 28.
181. Ibid.
182. Wikipedia, "Plano Senior High School."
183. Ibid., "T.W. Williams High School."
184. Ibid.
185. Benne, *Best High School Football in the Country*, 31.
186. Wikipedia, "John Clark Field."
187. PlanoFootball.com, "Stadium Info."
188. Benne, *Best High School Football in the Country*, 32.

Chapter 6

189. Ibid., 33.
190. Ibid., 34.
191. Ibid.
192. Ibid.
193. Interview by author, April 29, 2014.
194. Ibid.
195. Benne, *Best High School Football in the Country*, 35.
196. Ibid.
197. Holcomb, "Plano's *Friday Night Lights* Keeper Retires."
198. Ibid.
199. Ibid.
200. *Plano Star Courier*, "Haggards to Lead Cheers for Wildcats."
201. Friends of the Plano Public Library, *Plano, Texas*, 20.
202. http://lonestarfootball.net.
203. Ibid.
204. Ibid.
205. Ibid.
206. Ibid.
207. Interview by author, March 7, 2014.

208. Ibid.
209. Interview by author, April 29, 2014.
210. http://lonestarfootball.net.
211. Interview by author, March 7, 2014.
212. Benne, *Best High School Football in the Country*, 135.
213. Steve Christie Collection at Haggard Library in Plano, Texas.
214. Benne, *Best High School Football in the Country*, 135.
215. Ibid.
216. Benne, *Best High School Football in the Country*, 135.
217. Ibid.
218. Ibid.
219. Ibid., 136.
220. Ibid.
221. Interview by author, February 19, 2014.
222. http://lonestarfootball.net/.
223. Ibid.
224. Interview by author, February 19, 2014.
225. Hixson, King's Local Legacy."
226. Ibid.
227. Interview by author, February 19, 2014.
228. Ibid.

Chapter 7

229. Texas A&M University, "2013 Texas A&M Football Media Guide."
230. Interview by author, April 29, 2014.
231. Ibid.
232. Ibid.
233. Whitmire, "Handoffs."
234. Honea, *AHMO Power*.
235. McNabb, "Where But Texas?"
236. Mott, "Gerald Brence on the 70-30 Split."
237. Jiminez, "New Plano Coach Has 'Awesome Responsibility.'"
238. Interview by author, February 19, 2014.
239. Ibid.
240. Ibid.
241. Ibid.
242. Ibid.

BIBLIOGRAPHY

Advocate Mag. "40 Years of DISD Desegregation—Lakewood." http://lakewood.advocatemag.com/2011/07/22/a-gray-matter/.

Barron, David. "Stratford 1978 State Title Team Often Overlooked." *Houston Chronicle*, December 18, 2008.

Benne, Bart L. *The Best High School Football in the Country: A History of Plano, Texas High School Football from 1900 to the Present.* Dallas, TX: Taylor Pub., 1989.

Biel, Gail. "The Integration of Stephen F. Austin University." SFA Center for East Texas Studies. http://cets.sfasu.edu/story/subjects/Integration-Beil.html.

BlackPast.org. "Fort Worth, Texas, Where the West and the South Meet: A Brief History of the City's African American Community, 1849–2012." http://www.blackpast.org/perspectives/fort-worth-texas-where-west-and-south-meet-brief-history-citys-african-american-communi.

Campbell, Steve. "Tradition a Winner at Plano." *Fort Worth Star-Telegram*, December 15, 1986.

Dallas Morning News. "Lifelong McKinney Residents Recall Overcoming Segregation." http://www.dallasnews.com/news/community-news/mckinney/headlines/20140214-lifelong-mckinney-residents-recall-overcoming-segregation.ece.

———. "Quiet Man Set off Long, Loud Battle That Desegregated Dallas Schools." http://www.dallasnews.com/section-archives/125th-anniversary/headlines/20100806-quiet-man-set-off-long-loud-battle-that-desegregated-dallas-schools.ece.

———. "R.L. Turner Alumni Look Back on 50 Years Since Integration." http://www.dallasnews.com/news/community-news/carrollton-farmers-branch/headlines/20140214-r.l.-turner-alumni-look-back-on-50-years-since-integration.ece.

Examiner.com. "Early History of Plano, Texas." http://www.examiner.com/article/early-history-of-plano-texas.

Friends of the Plano Public Library. *Plano, Texas: The Early Years*. Wolfe City, TX: Henington, 1985.

Hageland, Kevin. "Losing a Legend: Plano, Mesquite Remember Tom Gray." Star Local Media, July 19, 2012. http://starlocalmedia.com/sports/losing-a-legend-plano-mesquite-remember-tom-gray/article_eafa70f3-2502-5294-b538-de4724d839c0.html.

Hasson, Devin. "Mesquite Football History: After a Tough Stretch, Skeets Back to Adding Winning Chapters to Story. Star Local Media, August 21, 2013. http://m.starlocalmedia.com/mesquitenews/sportsandsports/gridiron/mesquite-football-history-after-a-tough-stretch-skeeters-back-to/article_670975e3-1cc9-5273-9ecd-1f40d61b2532.html?mode=jqm.

High School Football Database. www.hsfdatabase.com.

Hixson, Josh. "King's Local Legacy: One of Positive Change." *Plano Star Courier*, January 13, 2007.

Holcomb, DeAnn. "Plano's *Friday Night Lights* Keeper Retires." *Plano Star Courier*, March 4, 2010.

Honea, Brian. *AHMO Power: The Story of the 1977 Texas 2A State Champion Wylie Pirates*. N.p.: iUniverse, 204.

Jiminez, David. "New Plano Coach Has 'Awesome Responsibility.'" *El Paso Times*, August 22, 2008.

Jones, Sharon. "Black History Month: University of Houston's Integration Story." Examiner.com, February 3, 2010. http://www.examiner.com/article/black-history-month-university-of-houston-s-integration-story.

Leszcynski, Ray. "Garland ISD's Changing Demographics Test Desegregation Plan." Dallas Morning News, July 19, 2013. http://www.dallasnews.com/news/community-news/garland-mesquite/headlines/20130719-garland-isds-changing-demographics-test-desegregation-plan.ece.

Lone Star Football Network. http://lonestarfootball.net.

McNabb, David. "Where But Texas Do 14,000 Show Up for 0-4 Team?" https://footballrecruiting.rivals.com/content.asp?CID=855001.

Mott, Britt. "Gerald Brence on the 70-30 Split." *Plano Profile*, January 2011.

Plano Conservancy for Historic Preservation, Inc. "Discovering Old Plano—An Historic Tour."

PlanoFootball.com. "Stadium Info." http://www.planofootball.com/gameday/stadium-info.

Plano Independent School District. "Kimbrough Ranked Among 'Top 10' Most Memorable Coaches in 50th Anniversary Texas Football Magazine." http://www.pisd.edu/news/archive/2009-10/kimbrough.shtml.

Plano Star Courier. "Haggards to Lead Cheers for Wildcats, Horned Frogs." August 7, 1968.

Powers, M. "Silent Transformation in the Bayou City: The Desegregation Process of Houston's Public Facilities." Houston Civil Rights Movement, April 9, 2012. http://houstoncivilrightsmovement.blogspot.com/2012/04/silent-transformation-in-bayou-city.html.

Pro-Football-Reference.com. "Pat Thomas." http://www.pro-football-reference.com/players/T/ThomPa00.htm.

Scarborough, Megan. "From Black and White to Color." UT Feature Story, October 9, 2008. http://www.utexas.edu/features/archive/2004/dorn.html.

Scott, Sam. "Hardaway Relates Tech Experience." Lubbock Online, July 2, 1999. http://lubbockonline.com/stories/020799/0207990053.shtml.

Smith, Corbett. "Playing in the Cotton Bowl on Grass Both a Treat and Challenge for Coaches, Players." *Dallas Morning News*, November 21, 2013. http://www.dallasnews.com/sports/high-schools/football-news/headlines/20131121-playing-in-the-cotton-bowl-on-grass-both-a-treat-and-challenge-for-coaches-players.ece.

Texas A&M University. "2013 Texas A&M Football Media Guide." http://www.aggieathletics.com/ViewArticle.dbml?ATCLID=208811560.

Texas State Historical Association. "MANSFIELD SCHOOL DESEGREGATION INCIDENT." http://www.tshaonline.org/handbook/online/articles/jcm02.

———. "PLANO, TX." https://www.tshaonline.org/handbook/online/articles/hdp04.

Thurman, Nita. "History of Integration: 50 Years of Change at North Texas." http://www.unt.edu/northtexan/archives/s04/history.htm.

Truesdell, Judy. "*Friday Night Lights* Star Returns to PISD." *Murphy Monitor*, January 28, 2009.

University of Houston. "UH at a Glance." http://www.uh.edu/about/uh-glance.

University of Texas. "Campus Profile." http://www.utexas.edu/about-ut/campus-profile.

Whitmire, Keith. "Handoffs: Swap Meets Still Work for Exchanging Game Videos in Football." *Dallas Morning News*, October 23, 2008.

Wikipedia. "Brown v. Board of Education." http://en.wikipedia.org/wiki/Brown_v._Board_of_Education.

———. "Historical Events of Houston." http://en.wikipedia.org/wiki/Historical_events_of_Houston.

———. "Houston." http://en.wikipedia.org/wiki/Houston.

———. "John Clark Field." http://en.wikipedia.org/wiki/John_Clark_Field.

———. "Lubbock, Texas." http://en.wikipedia.org/wiki/Lubbock%2C_Texas.

———. "Plano Senior High School." http://en.wikipedia.org/wiki/Plano_Senior_High_School.

———. "Plano, Texas." http://en.wikipedia.org/wiki/Plano,_Texas.

———. "T.H. Williams High School." http://en.wikipedia.org/wiki/T._H._Williams_High_School.

YouTube. "Annie Heads Rainwater—Mini Documentary 2012." https://www.youtube.com/watch?v=v3KzJxaw2kU.

INDEX

M

N

P

R

S

T

U

W

ABOUT THE AUTHORS

Jeffrey C. Campbell is the co-director for the Plano Conservancy for Historic Preservation, Inc. He has a degree in heritage resources with a concentration in historic preservation from Northwestern State University of Louisiana. He has worked on historic preservation projects in Texas,

From left to right: Amy Crawford, Kirby Stokes and Jeff Campbell. *Courtesy of Mike Newman.*

Louisiana and New Mexico. He is also a published folk poet and writes a column for Stephen F. Austin State University's Center for Regional Heritage Research. He lives in McKinney, Texas, with his wife, Rhenda Gray.

Amy Sandling Crawford was raised in Plano, Texas. She graduated from Plano East Senior High School and has a degree in journalism with public relations emphasis from the University of North Texas. A widely published journalist and successful public relations specialist, Amy uses her talents to promote many nonprofits, businesses and community groups in Plano and beyond. She lives in Plano with her husband, Ben, and their daughter, Elizabeth Grace.

Kirby Stokes is a student at the University of Texas–Dallas pursuing her graduate degree in History. She was raised in north Dallas and currently resides in Allen, Texas. She lives with her wonderful husband, Alex Lindsey, and their rambunctious dog, Marley.

About the Plano Conservancy for Historic Preservation, Inc.

The Plano Conservancy for Historic Preservation, Inc. is a Texas-based nonprofit organization dedicated to promoting civic pride in the past, increasing preservation awareness through education and public outreach and providing financial assistance to protect and preserve our heritage resources for current and future generations. The Plano Conservancy for Historic Preservation, Inc. is especially focused on preserving the history and heritage of Plano, Texas. www.planoconservancy.org.